MAGIC
MUCK

Raised Catholic
(Can You Tell?)

❖ ❖ ❖

"Stivender's storytelling emanates from a warm,
familial setting and resonates with affectionate
humor while he takes swipes at the rites of
passage of a more innocent time.
These tales amuse while they recall a humor
shared by many."
— **PUBLISHERS WEEKLY**

❖ ❖ ❖

"A feast of good feelings."
— **KIRKUS REVIEWS**

❖ ❖ ❖

"Stivender has lent his storytelling gift to a work
that combines two wonderful inside jokes—
growing up Catholic and growing up in the 1950s.
Hootus est. (Latin for 'it's a hoot.')"
— **Kevin O'Brian, THE PLAIN DEALER**

❖ ❖ ❖

"Charming . . . The story of his first day
of first grade at Holy Cross School
is almost worth the price of the book itself."
— **John Corr, PHILADELPHIA INQUIRER**

MAGIC MUCK

The Complete Guide to Compost

Lady Muck

ILLUSTRATED BY TIM COATH

To Mum and Dad with love

I'd like to thank everyone who has supported Lady Muck over the years, from
those early heady days to these crazy enigmatic times. You know who you
are; I can't mention you all personally. But this book is a testament to your
kindness and friendship, for without it there would have been no book, no
story and no business. My thanks also to Emma, Trevor and the 'team' at
Pavilion for their help and infectious enthusiasm in realizing my ambition to
write *Magic Muck*.

First published in Great Britain in 1994 by
PAVILION BOOKS LIMITED
26 Upper Ground, London SE1 9PD

Text copyright © Jane Down 1994
Illustrations copyright © Tim Coath 1994

The moral right of the author has been asserted.

Designed by Nigel Partridge

A CIP catalogue record for this book
is available from the British Library.

ISBN 1 85793 2617 (hbk)
ISBN 1 85793 3923 (pbk)

Filmset by Selwood Systems, Midsomer Norton
Printed and bound in Great Britain by Butler & Tanner Ltd, Frome

2 4 6 8 10 9 7 5 3 1

This book may be ordered by post
direct from the publisher. Please contact
the Marketing Department.
But try your bookshop first.

CONTENTS

CHAPTER ONE

SHOVELLING THE PROVERBIAL

The cure for the ill, is not to sit still
Nor froust with a book by the fire
But to take a large hoe and a shovel also
And dig till you gently perspire

RUDYARD KIPLING (1865–1936)

I wonder how many people come home to find a message on their answering machines asking if they would be interested in writing a book on muck. Well that is exactly what happened to me (what a thing to ask a lady), and this book is living proof of it.

Having had a wonderful half-page spread in *The Times* one weekend – I'm a devil for publicity – I was contacted by a chap who thought the article, although not written by me, was a perfect base for a new book all about compost. And who better to write it than Lady Muck herself. Just think, not since the *Muck Manual* of 1843 has there been such a concise, informative and, I do hope, amusing account of compost, muck et al.

You could say that, as a Somerset farmer's daughter, I cut my first tooth on a dung heap; well, it was a sandpit actually, but ever since then my parents have had an awful job to keep me away from all things mucky. A career in compost wasn't exactly what I had in mind when I was at school, although I wanted to be involved in agriculture. As it was, I ended up doing all sorts of things, including being a nanny, a waitress, a barmaid and a cook, before going, for a spell, to agricultural college to do a farm secretarial course. From there I moved to a job behind a desk overlooking the goods entrance of a branch of Marks & Spencer. The only advantage of this was that I did get a preview of things to come.

After a couple of years I got fed up with my desk job, and my father offered me an alternative – milking the cows on a farm he had just acquired for my brother, who then decided to go off to college and get some qualifications. I jumped at the opportunity (little realizing at the time that when my brother came home I wouldn't have a job).

Shortly afterwards, while my brother was away at college, we had a pollution problem at the home farm. Three watercourses cross our land, converging to make one river that runs through the nearby village, and we have always had to be very careful to avoid spreading muck in such a way as to contaminate the local water supply. My father, realizing the potential risk, had always consulted the Water Board for advice on drainage systems, collection tanks etc. Unfortunately, one dry summer some muck seeped into an old stone drain put in by farmers in Victorian times, thence into one of our three watercourses and on into the river, causing a minor incidence of pollution. New legislation on water contamination had been introduced and the Water Board had no option but to take us to court.

However, the judge decided that, because my father had always followed the Water Board's advice to the letter and had spent a lot of money on new drainage systems and collection tanks, it didn't seem fair to fine him. He was ordered to pay court costs instead (which, lo and behold, happened to be the equivalent of the fine at that time).

Upset by the whole ordeal, father decided to look around at new machinery which could perhaps help solve his pollution problem. At first he was led to believe that he could put a lid on our above-ground slurry store (I'm sure you have all seen those huge, dark blue-green circular tanks on farms – and they are not swimming-pools as one or two people tend to think). Putting a lid on the slurry store and allowing the muck to bubble inside would produce, we were told, methane gas, which could be used to run a generator supplying electricity to the farm; not only that, but the bubbling effect would help to evaporate the muck and we would be left with a third of the original amount. Sounded wonderful: free electricity at one end, reduced waste at the other. Even at a cost of tens of thousands of pounds, it had to be the answer to all our prayers. However, things were not as they seemed. For a start, we were not going to get all this wonderful free electricity since cows have a slight problem. It is called belching and burping and most of their methane gas goes out at the wrong end. Pigs, on the other hand, produce vast quantities of the stuff. It goes out at the right end, but we don't have any pigs. As to the evaporation of muck, well, that was just a load of old codswallop: you had the same amount of muck at the end of the day as you did at the beginning. So the whole idea was thrown out of the window.

Then father was taken to see a machine called a slurry separator, which had been invented by three farmers, two from Somerset and one from Oxfordshire. All had been fined for pollution by their water boards, and they had got together to try and devise a system to control pollution problems on the farm. To consolidate their ideas they went first to Denmark and Holland where, as a result of extremely intensive farming practices, the disposal of muck has created enormous problems. Now I am sure that most of you, especially if you are 'Archers' fans, know all about the various quotas that have been imposed on farmers in recent years: sheep, beef, potato, milk – you name it, we have it! Well, almost. For the Dutch and Danes have taken it one step further and introduced the Muck Quota. Should a farmer, or rather his animals, produce more muck than is stipulated by the quota, they will be fined or levied in much the same way as a farmer who overproduces milk, for example. What are we coming to? They now have muck co-operatives in Denmark and Holland. Muck is collected from farms by tanker and taken to the nearest co-operative, where it is mixed with muck from all sorts of livestock systems – dairy, beef, pig, chicken – and this wonderful concoction is then put in a very modern and efficient methane digester. The methane gas is used to produce electricity, some of which now supplies their national grid, and the residue is sold to the Dutch horticultural industry.

These three chaps pooled their ideas and invented the slurry separator, and my father was one of the very first farmers in the country to have one installed. Before it was delivered a large area of concrete had to be laid so that tractors and trailers could easily drive round the machine. A lovely, gleaming pad of white concrete was duly laid. Then father, thinking that the separator was bound to turn up when he wasn't there and would be put in the wrong place, had a large circle marked out on the concrete to indicate exactly where it was to go. Now the nearby village, sitting on a hill, overlooks our home farm. When the villagers saw the concrete being laid they thought nothing of it but, when the circle was marked out, word went round like wildfire that 'old Downie' (as my father is known) was getting a helicopter, and was taking to the skies to visit all his farms. When we heard this we just couldn't resist telling them that the helicopter would not be delivered until the control tower arrived, and that really got them going. A farmer with a control tower! Whatever next? In fact, when the slurry separator was installed, I suppose it did look like a control tower of sorts. Standing on four legs, twenty feet (6m) high, it was a nine-foot (2.7-m) square, battleship-grey hut, complete with window, door, stairwell and red and green lights – an instant control tower.

The idea of the machine is to separate the muck from our cows into a solid and a liquid, making it considerably easier to handle. A cow produces on average about nineteen gallons (85 lit.) of muck a day. Compared with a human, who produces an average of about twenty-nine gallons (130 lit.) of waste in a day, through baths, washing-up etc, this is, I suppose, a mere drop in the ocean. With the separator came an irrigation system which works in conjunction with it. The dirty liquid from the separator is collected in a tank and used to irrigate the fields, the irrigator being moved from one field to the next as the farmer sees fit. This system is not only beneficial to the land in that it does not cause any pollution problems, but it also means that we avoid spreading slurry at the wettest time of the year. If we tear up the fields with tractors and heavy slurry tankers, compacting the soil and generally making an awful mess, we have to spend a lot of time, and a lot of money, recultivating that field in the spring. When you hear about the pollution of watercourses by farm slurry, what has actually happened is that the deoxygenating bacteria, which stick to the solid matter in the slurry, have deprived the watercourses, and all the life they contain, of oxygen. Silage effluent is extremely potent because of its acerbic nature, and so is pig slurry, but apparently the worst thing for pollution is milk due to its biological oxygen demand.

The waste or solids which are produced by the slurry separator resemble a fresh green horse manure: very fibrous, no smell

and really quite pleasant to handle. The farmers who had designed the separator told my father that he would be able to sell the waste to local parks, nurseries or garden centres. He tried this, but to no avail. The problem of living in the West Country is that the farms produce so much muck that we can't even give the stuff away.

The installation of the separator had coincided with my brother coming back from agricultural college. By then I felt that I wanted a change from agriculture anyway, so I started looking in all the newspapers and magazines for a wonderful, interesting job; as long as it combined travel, glamour and meeting people I was going to do it. However, this coincided with the recession of 1986 and work was difficult to come by. After a couple of months of job hunting I happened to go out on the farm one day, the separator had been performing its task and a huge pile of solids had built up on the concrete. I asked my father what he was going to do with it as he couldn't sell it. Nor could he use it on the fields as the solid matter would act like a mulch and kill off the grass; not only that, but if it rained heavily the solids would be washed off the fields and back into the watercourses, and then we would be back at square one again. I mentioned to my father that, having watched the gardening programmes on television lately and read various articles in gardening magazines, I had gathered that gardeners were crying out for this sort of material. Full of humus and nutrient, it was just what they wanted. So why didn't father compost the solids, bag them and sell them to the gardeners? My father then suggested to me that, as I was looking for an exciting job, wanted to travel and meet people, I should set up my own business and try selling the muck myself. I was horrified. How could my father suggest to his only daughter that she shovel the proverbial for the rest of her life? However, after a couple of weeks I decided that I had to do something, so I went round the garden centres and asked very tentatively if they would be receptive to the idea. In fact one or two told me that when I was ready to start selling I should go back and see them as they would be most interested in the end product. So that was how I came to be involved in the muck business.

In November of 1986 I started composting in earnest, to be ready for the spring market of 1987, but I still didn't have a name for my product. Having looked at all the various composts available and studied their brand names, I decided that if I was going to succeed I had to find a name that would be catchy, describe the product aptly and make people smile. What a combination. In the end it was my mother who accidentally came up with the answer. Every morning I would go out to my compost heaps and turn them over, shred the compost and then mix it with sphagnum moss peat in the right proportions to make a versatile, truly natural product for the gardener. Later in the morning I would go into see Mum for a cup of coffee, and every morning without fail she would jokingly say, 'Morning Lady Muck, and what's it like on the compost heap today?' After a bit this wore pretty thin but the words 'Lady Muck' caught my imagination. I said I thought Lady Muck would be a wonderful name for the product, and for the business. It described the product well, it is a household name, and it would liven up every gardener's day. My mother wasn't too happy about the name, to say the least. She thought I might offend one or two people, but, as I pointed out to her, in this day and age you can be called something a darned sight worse than Lady Muck. So my mother's nick-name for me was adopted in earnest, though unfortunately it has backfired on her. When I go away on business she runs the office for me and answers the phone. In the early days, if people asked if they were speaking to Lady Muck, my mother would reply that it was in fact Lady Muck's mother, and could she help. As you can imagine, this would lead to guffaws of laughter down the phone before an order was placed. After several years my mother decided that she was getting fed up with being known as Lady Muck's mother; after all, for the last thirty-odd years she had been known as John Down's wife. Why couldn't she be known as something in her own right? Well one day she mentioned this to a garden centre who had rung up to place an order. They agreed that she should have a status of her own rather than being known as John Down's wife or Lady Muck's mother, and they offered to help solve the problem. Several days later they rang back with the news that they had come up with an answer: from now on, they

had decided to call mother 'Duchess Dung', the 'Duchess' for short.

For making my compost, and I produce hundreds and hundreds of tons a year, I follow the traditional composting process that has been with us for hundreds if not thousands of years. Aeration is the most important factor in any compost heap (more of this in Chapter Three). Every week the heaps of solids from the separator are turned, aerating the compost and allowing the bacteria to breathe. They in turn work away faster at the cellulose material, breaking it down and, in so doing, creating heat. This heat – and our heaps get up to 150 degrees Fahrenheit (approximately 65 degrees centigrade) – ensures that any weed seeds are sterilized and any toxic pathogens neutralized, should they be present. After twelve to fourteen weeks the heat of the heaps falls to an ambient temperature of around 70 degrees Fahrenheit (21 degrees centigrade). By then all the material in the heap has been thoroughly cooked, and is now ready to blend with another substrate in order to reinforce its versatility for the gardener.

Originally we were going to sell the composted manure just as it was. But because of its high moisture content, the compost tended to compact and we had to blend it with something entirely natural to absorb the excessive moisture. We found that many people didn't want just a straight composted manure for their gardens; they wanted something that was not only an excellent soil conditioner but a planting medium, fertilizer and top dressing as well. Having tried many materials, including chopped straw, sawdust (of which there is a percentage in the compost anyway because it forms the cows' bedding), sedge peat and sphagnum moss peat, it was the latter that gave our product the consistency and quality that we had been looking for. (Before all you anti-peat demons shut this book and vow never to open its pages again, at least read Chapter Five 'Muck through the Ages', which gives the history of peat and its uses in the garden: you will find it enlightening.) A minimal amount of Irish moss peat is used for making Lady Muck compost, approximately twenty per cent weight for weight, which in comparison with other products on the market is very minimal. The beauty of sphagnum moss peat is its dryness. It absorbs all the excess moisture from the cow compost and, more importantly, absorbs all the nutrients as well, so it is a very valuable ingredient of the final product. The peat also opens up the compost and makes it friable, allowing air movement, which all plants need. Just because they are in the ground, a bit

like worms, doesn't necessarily mean that they don't need air. The peat and compost mixture goes through another composting process for approximately a month and then is passed through a shredder. From there it goes to a bagging machine, into a bag, on to a pallet and away to the distributor.

The equipment that I have today is certainly a far cry from what I had when I first started off all those years ago. I couldn't afford a bagging machine then, or indeed much else in the way of equipment, and all the composting was done by hand. It was just me, my shovel and a bucket. For the first two years every bag that was sold was filled by hand: four and a half two-gallon (9-lit.) bucketfuls to the bag. However, before I began to look too much like Quasimodo's sister, I was able to acquire a small bagging machine, which relieved me of most of the back-breaking work, although I was still shovelling the proverbial by hand. You should see some of my old shovels.

I have learnt over the years that the easiest part of the business is making the product; the hardest part is selling it. When I first started, cold calling at garden centres was the order of the day. I would arrive complete with samples and sales spiel but found that this just wasn't enough. The garden centres always wanted more. So desperate was I to get an order one day that, having gone through my 'routine', I mentioned to the manager that I would do an 'in-store promotion'. (I had no idea what an in-store promotion was; it just sounded good.) The manager suddenly became very interested. 'What do you do?' he asked. My mind suddenly went into overdrive and, looking around, my eyes came to rest on my logo, showing a supercilious-looking woman wearing a hat covered in fruit and veg. 'Oh, I dress up as Lady Muck, I wear a hat covered in fruit and veg, and I'll hold a free raffle and give away bags of Lady Muck.' 'Wonderful!' came the reply; 'I'll have two pallets, and can you come along two weeks on Saturday and spend the day with us?' How could I refuse? I walked out of that garden centre on cloud nine, but came down to earth with a bump when I realized I had a slight problem. Where on earth was I going to find a hat covered with fruit and veg? I spent the following fortnight searching through every hat shop in Somerset for the perfect hat, but to no avail. I then came to the conclusion that I was going to have to make my own. I managed to get hold of one of those folding sunhats with a wire rim, and found that it held a garland of fruit and veg extremely well. That was it. Every weekend and bank holiday for the next few years you could find me promoting my product in garden centres throughout the south and east of England. I am glad to say that, after a few years, I was able to afford to have a hat made, covered with silk fruit and vegetables, which I now wear only to open garden centres or flower shows. I just don't have the time any more to do in-store promotions, although they were extremely successful and really put Lady Muck on the map. I have now given over one hundred talks nationwide, to gardening clubs, WIs, Retirement Associations, any group you care to name. I have even had to research a second talk because my first one, 'On the Way to the Compost Heap', was so popular that clubs wanted me back again but asked if I could speak about something else. Of course I could. With a good drop of Irish blood in my veins, I should be able to talk the hind leg off a donkey. 'The Life and Times of a Georgian Gardener' became my next theme; indeed, its subject matter is another love of my life.

When muck is your passion and worms are your favourite creatures (more about these in Chapter Four), you are bound to attract a bit of attention, especially if you are female. It's just not the done thing to go running round the countryside, thrusting your hands into other people's dung heaps to verify the quality of their manure. Obviously, this unusual occupation has attracted the media's attention – television, radio, newspapers and magazines have all done features on Lady Muck – and the name has caught the public's imagination. It has all been great fun. It's no good doing something unless you are happy, and I am happy – poor but happy. My only real claim to fame is that I am probably the only person in the farming and horticultural community who has had a chance to assault John Gummer, then Minister of Agriculture. He caught wind of what I was doing down here in deepest, darkest Somerset, and during a visit to the West Country he suggested coming to see me at work. Unfortunately, I had a trade show in Exeter that day, but, as he was such an important guest, I rushed back home to meet him, donning all the Lady Muck gear, including the hat. He dug into my heaps of compost, not too willing to withdraw his hands from such delightful material, and then crouched over my bags to read them. As I leant over him to answer a question, I lost my footing, a plastic cucumber fell from the hat and doffed him on the head. Mr Gummer was quite stunned for a moment, obviously no one had ever hit the Minister of Agriculture before. Then he said, so surprised, 'I've just been hit on the head with a plastic cucumber'. As none of the press were present at that moment, he grabbed the cucumber and ran out of the shed, shouting, 'Lady Muck's just hit me on the head with a plastic cucumber', at which everyone cheered and applauded. I did apologise for the offence but, as I pointed out to him, it could have been worse: I might have fallen on him instead and suffocated him. Well now, there's a thought.

Anyway, enough of my trials and tribulations. This is supposed to be a book about compost, manure and all things bountiful. So, come with me, travelling through time from past to present, and share those delights that all we compost makers aspire to.

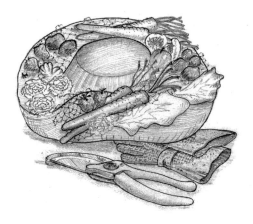

CHAPTER TWO

IN THE BEGINNING THERE WAS SOIL . . .

To see a world in a grain of sand
And a heaven in a wild flower
Hold infinity in the palm of your hand
And eternity in an hour

WILLIAM BLAKE (1757–1827)

*H*aving read many books on soil and its structure, it's a wonder that I wasn't put off writing about this magnificent giver of life. I found most books were too technical, and all I want to do in this chapter is give you a taster – if that is the right word – of the soil and how you can help nurture it for the benefit of your garden. As many of you are probably aware, different soils are found all over this country and, no matter where you live, it seems that someone, somewhere, is always complaining about it, just like the weather. You're never happy with what you've got. But if you realized how much time it has taken for the soil to form, and how many processes have been involved, you might just think twice before another outburst about cracked clays and greedy sands. They all have a part to play, but you can in any case, with a bit of effort, alter your soil for the better.

My earliest experience of soils and their formation was as a child, when my two brothers and I embarked on an adventure down by the stream about half a mile from the farm where we lived. My elder brother had been given a tent for his birthday, and, as we were obsessed with cowboys and Indians, we decided to make a camp just like the cowboys. We were also determined to have a fire – one of those lovely, smoke-free stone circles that you see in every Western – and cook beans and sausages and make coffee. We even made pots and plates out of the clay that was to be found in large quantities by the stream, and perched them precariously on top of the circle of stones. We got the fire going but couldn't understand why it was so smokey. This didn't happen to John Wayne. As the fire got hotter, so did our adventure, for the stones that we used to encase the fire were flints, and under the enormous heat they started to split. And it didn't stop there. It was just as

17

though someone had emptied a box full of fireworks onto the fire. The flints whistled passed our ears, smashing our clay crockery, and the dog, giving up on this meal, could be heard yelping all the way home. We decamped pretty quickly, but for several hours these flints provided us with a terrific firework display. John Wayne's reputation really went down the pan for us children, especially when our parents told us that the fires we saw in the films were gas fires on set, hence the smoke-free environment. Looking back on this adventure, I suppose I can say that I witnessed the effects of weathering and the first stage in the formation of soil, although it was going to take a lot of camp fires and a few hundred thousand years to complete the process.

Soil can be likened to the family heirloom. No I am not mad. It really is a priceless inheritance, and if you have anything of historic value in your home, you take care of it. You polish it with love and place it for all to see. Likewise, with the soil in your garden, one of life's natural antiques, it must be nurtured and cared for. Treated carefully, it will repay you many times over in the years to come. Everyone knows that the family heirloom, if neglected, falls into disrepair and loses its lustre. So too does the soil if it is not treated with the same respect. Soil is precious, the most valuable commodity in your garden. But where does it come from? What determines the type of soil in your garden? What magical properties does it contain? And how can you make the most of it?

Soil was formed many thousands if not millions of years ago, and it is still being formed today. The lavas that were thrown up through early volcanic activity eventually cooled down and solidified, and then through erosion by means of rain, wind, ice, frost and heat from the sun, these rocks were eventually worn away. Rock and mineral particles from the mountains were washed down by rains to the valleys below, where they were swept along by fast-flowing rivers. They were then deposited, together with the remains of all forms of sea life, as the rivers flowed at a slower pace across the lowland plains. There they formed thick layers of sediment, which became compressed under the weight of yet more rock particles and the remains of sea creatures. These layers have eventually become new rocks, and over the years the earth's movements have raised these layers out of the water so that they have formed new land, which has then been eroded once more by the elements, and the cycle has started all over again. Apparently much of this country has been submerged at least twice, some areas four times or more. A new layer of rock has been formed each time, and these layers, or strata, pile up on top of each other like a huge sandwich. Had these layers remained undisturbed, the landscape of this planet would have been rather flat and featureless, with small rises where the original rock was still in the process of weathering. Today, much of Britain slopes towards the east. The rock formation along the east coast is weak, or soft, and the action of waves from the North Sea battering against these rocks is now eroding this land at a terrific pace. Rocks to the west of Britain are much harder and resistant, and they rise up to form the Cotswolds, the Pennines, the moors of the West Country and the mountains of western Scotland and Wales.

Many of you are, I am sure, aware of the variety of soils in your gardens. This is due to the movement of glaciers over this land during the various ice ages. The weight and movement of the ice ground down the rocks over which it travelled, and, as each glacier receded with the onset of a warmer period in the earth's history, these fragments, some minute, some extremely large, were deposited in valleys carved out by the glaciers. Finer particles of rock were washed away by the melting glacial waters, leaving behind gravels, stones and sands. There were several glacial periods in this country; at the end of the third the encroaching glacier came to rest along the Cotswolds and Chilterns, extending from the River Severn to the Thames. This may explain the variety of soils to be found in the south of England, from the West Country through to Essex. Hertfordshire really has a mixed bag of soils, due to the effect of icy sludge under the glacier which covered this county. When it melted, the rivers that formed picked up sediment which they deposited along their course, leaving behind stretches of clay here, gravel there and sand somewhere else. In the fourth glacial period the ice came to rest along a line stretching from the Severn Valley to York. For quite some time after the ice had melted Britain must have looked like a huge quagmire, with an underlying layer of permafrost, or semi-frozen subsoil. As this huge quagmire dried out, various plants took hold, firstly mosses and willows. As the climate warmed up, other plants were introduced from the Continent. Birch trees made an appearance, followed by pine, hazel, elm and oak. In about 5000 BC conditions became warmer still, and lime and elder were introduced. It was through the action of ice that our soils, formed by rock fragments, enabled the forests to get a foothold. The trees of these forests contributed a whole new element to the soil: humus. As they died, their remains added food, energy and organic matter to the soil, completing its formation and creating ideal conditions in which a whole host of living organisms could flourish. As they in turn acted upon the soil, they produced an ideal habitat for plants, and from this we benefit today. It was around this time that the narrow stretch of lowland separating us from the Continent was finally breached and Britain became an island.

Man, in the form of Paleolithic hunters, came here around 2500 BC, but it was Neolithic man who brought cereals, and various weeds to boot. Much of this country was covered in forest and small areas were cultivated for food, but it wasn't until Roman times that larger areas were cleared for crops. Although prehistoric man had managed to clear the scrub and rough vegetation on the chalky downs and in the sandy valleys, it was the Romans who started large-scale deforestation. There are thought to have been around one and a half million people living in this country then and, to feed them, an area of around two million acres was required. Unfortunately, the techniques that the Romans brought with them were abandoned after the fall of the Roman Empire; the cultivation of Britain then fell into decline and the land reverted to forest and scrub. Up until the early part of the last century only relatively small areas of land had been cleared for more than 1500 years, which was not enough time for a marked change. Today, the story is quite different. Since the introduction of the 'cheap food policy' after the Second World War, all manner of different methods of cultivation have been employed, along with fertilizers and pesticides, and these have had a profound effect on the soil, its stability and fertility. Large-scale clearing for intensive farming practices to feed our ever-increasing population have put paid to a healthy soil. In some areas erosion of exposed, bare land by wind and rain has had a marked effect on soil quality and quantity. Many arable farmers have experienced this type of erosion, mainly as a result of leaving land bare for several months during the winter, with no plant life to hold the soil in place; it therefore becomes vulnerable to the elements. But it's not all doom and gloom: in many areas the soil is probably more fertile today than it has ever been. The large amounts of both human and animal waste that have to be disposed of are now being applied to the land. Many farmers and horticulturalists are realizing the folly of always following the guidelines set out by the various fertilizer companies and the

Ministry of Agriculture during the past thirty-odd years, who encouraged the use of chemicals and artificial fertilizers, and the key issue today is soil health and the level of humus in the soil.

John Evelyn, seventeenth-century horticulturalist and arbori-culturalist extraordinaire and a prolific writer, wrote a book about the soil called *Terra*. In this early work he declared that there were reckoned to be no less than 'one hundred and seventy-nine million one thousand and sixty different sorts of Earths'. I think he could be right. No garden, however small, consists of only one type of soil: the earth is a mixture of soils with an underlying predominance of one particular type.

The soil is made up of various constituents: mineral matter, organic matter, air, water and soil organisms. The mineral content of the soil has come from various rocks through erosion, and these rocks are divided into three types:

Igneous These were formed by volcanic activity and are the oldest rocks known to man. They consist of such rocks as granite and basalt and are found mainly in the north and west of Britain, extending northwards from the south-west peninsular, through Wales to the north-west of England and thence to the Highlands of Scotland.

Sedimentary These rocks were formed by fragments of igneous rocks which were deposited under water, together with the remains of sea life. As the layers became compressed they formed the rocks that we know as sandstone, limestone, shale and dolomite.

Metamorphic These were formed when heat and pressure were applied to igneous and sedimentary rocks, converting granite into gneiss, limestone into marble and shales into slate.

Minerals are the main ingredient of rock formation. Those of you who wish to be one up on your neighbours and become an expert on soil will have to know the different types of rocks from which soil is formed. An analysis of the individual earth particles will determine not only what type of soil you have, for example clay or sand, but also its nutrient content, how it will behave in response to the elements and, more importantly, what plants you can grow in your garden. But before all you budding pedologists throw away your soil testing kits after taking a quick sample from the garden, there is more to this than meets the eye. I hadn't really intended to go this far down the garden path on the subject of soils but now that I am here I might as well share my information with you.

Ninety per cent of the earth's crust is made up of minerals, and these can be divided into two main groups:

Silica This mineral is extremely hard and it is only with great difficulty that it can be ground down into a fine powder or dust. Quartz, flints and sandstones come under the silica heading. Sand is derived from sandstone which has been attacked by rainwater (a very dilute acid), whose action dissolves the adhesive agent that binds this mineral together.

Silicate This is formed when silicon, oxygen and other elements are combined. Silicates are rather a mixed bunch of minerals, some of which are as hard as sand and resistant to the elements, while others decompose readily under the effects of rain water. Those silicates that do break down easily form new compounds which contain many of the elements vital for healthy plant growth, such as potassium, magnesium, calcium, iron, aluminium and sodium.

When land is cleared for the building of a housing estate the building contractors usually sell off the loamy topsoil to parks and public gardens, leaving the incoming gardener with a rough patch of subsoil. On quite a few up-market estates the gardens are now turfed over but, more often than not, they are left uncultivated and stripped of topsoil, ensuring many

years of hard work ahead for the gardener in replacing that lovely humic layer. But don't despair, all is not lost. If you have a new garden then at least you have the wonderful opportunity of improving the soil conditions, which in most cases will be a darned sight easier than moving into a property whose garden has been totally neglected, leaving impoverished soil, weeds running riot and crumbling walls and garden paths.

The only part of the soil that the gardener would normally come into contact with is the topsoil. It's rare to find ourselves digging down into the depths of our gardens unless we are building an extension to the house, creating a large pond or a drainage system for that permanently wet patch – or because, perish the thought, the family pet pony has died and is to be given pride of place eight feet down underneath the vegetable patch. Some people recommend that if you acquire a new garden it is advisable to dig down several feet to see just what the subsoil is like, since this would give you a good indication of the nature of the topsoil, especially as regards its drainage properties. The fact of the matter is that the topsoil really is the most important factor in producing a beautiful fertile garden; this is the wonderful material on which your garden and its plants are going to rely, and the health and constituency of this soil is all-important.

The topsoil, which is sometimes known as the litter or humus layer, is the end result of many years of decomposition of organic material that has been worked upon by various bodies, such as bacteria, worms, insects and fungi, and has been combined with mineral rock fragments. The subsoil underneath consists of a layer of stony, gritty soil, and if you dig a little deeper you will find clay or gravel and eventually, deeper still, the base rock. This does not apply to all gardens in this country; on the contrary, those that answer this description are the property of very fortunate gardeners. Most of us, regrettably, have the litter layer, a few inches of stones and then heavy clay. I speak from experience. I don't even recall ever seeing the base rock, the clay is so deep in our part of Somerset. Occasionally it's the other way round: a shallow, stony topsoil and below it solid rock, especially on the chalk downs. My sympathies are with the victims of these conditions too.

There are basically five different types of soil: clay, chalk and limestone, sand, loam, and peat and fen. Although most soils are a mixture of one or two of the above types, there are various factors involved when it comes to identifying them.

CLAY SOILS

It greets a' winter and girns a' summer

DR JOHN BROWN

At one time you could tell when you had entered a clay district: perhaps there were brickworks, broad grassy vales, oak woods and forests, the famous fox-hunting vales or, down in Cornwall, the white clay extracted for use in china manufacture. Today it's a little different. With modern farming and gardening techniques, rejuvenation and moulding of soils is now achieved without much physical effort. When wet clay is rubbed between the fingers it feels smooth and silky, although quite sticky to the touch. This is the soil that gives you 'platform wellies' should you venture out on the garden during wet weather. Clay soils are normally cold and heavy. They are called 'cold' soils because of their composition: the mineral fragments they contain are extremely small and they compact together, prohibiting the passage of air and limiting the drainage of water through the soil. This lowers the soil temperature. When the sun shines, the warm air also takes a long time to circulate and heat the soil. When it does, it has a wonderful tendency to dry it out completely, and you are left with a huge pad of cracked concrete. And that is not all: because the clay acts like a sponge in absorbing the water so efficiently, it tends to prevent the plants in the soil from extracting water themselves. This causes them to wilt, even though there is probably adequate water for them. You just can't win. The term 'heavy' refers to its working properties; being sticky and cold, clay tends to clog up machinery and garden tools, and, because of its wetness, it's like trying to move a gigantic sponge sodden with water. On the positive side, clays are essential for forming tilth, or loams, since they hold together fine, sandy particles which would otherwise just dry out and form sandpits. They also have a very important chemical property known as base exchange, which is peculiar to clay. Each clay particle is surrounded by a glue-like material containing 'bases', which are the elements of calcium, potassium, magnesium, hydrogen and sodium. The most beneficial aspect of these base exchanges is demonstrated when fertilizer is added to the soil. The fertilizer, for example sulphate of potash, which is a soluble salt, will be exchanged by the bases for potassium, which then becomes fixed by the clay. The potassium will not leach out of the soil if the plant doesn't require it, but will be retained by the clay bases until a need for potassium arises. Because of this marvellous system, clay soils are ideal plant food providers.

For many centuries the only way to enrich clay soils was to add manure from dung heaps or, if they were unavailable, to add lime or chalk. The manure would add body and introduce bacteria to the soil, which would awaken it from its dormant state, help with drainage and supply valuable nutrients for the next crop. Lime or chalk has been used for many years as it makes the clay less sticky and opens up the soil, allowing movement of water through it; it also gives the clay particles access to air and therefore a chance to dry out. Clay soils tend to be acidic. The addition of lime neutralizes this acidity, allowing a wider range of plants to be grown. One favourite way of dealing with clay soils is to dig them in the autumn and leave the soil bare during the winter in order that frosts can act upon the clay, freezing and thawing it by turns so that in spring it should just fall apart and form a lovely rich tilth. For best results, dig the soil and incorporate plenty of good organic matter. This will double the benefits come the spring.

CHALK AND LIMESTONE SOILS

More often than not these two types of soil are lumped together under the heading of either chalk or lime. Although they are quite similar and need the same treatment, they are quite unalike in their formation. Limestone is the result of layers of sediment formed by the skeletons of corals, which thrived in the warm waters around Britain millions of years ago. Chalk is formed by the skeletons of other marine organisms which lived in our clear seas around the same time. When these died they settled on the sea bed and were compressed by further layers of sediment, which crushed their skeletons and formed chalk.

Beech trees thrive in both lime and chalk areas and, in the clay valleys of limestone hills, streams spring forth to give life to the land. Many settlements were established at the feet of limestone hills, and lime kilns were built in these areas to produce quicklime for farmers and cement for builders. The chalk plains of Salisbury in Wiltshire, over which I have travelled on numerous occasions, have always been renowned for their wheat crops and sheep grazing, and today the odd free-range pig and his hut can also be seen here. But I suppose the most obvious sign of living in a limestone area is the hard water. The kettle in my kitchen has more 'fur' than some of the local rabbits.

Chalk and lime soils do not present too many problems, unlike clays. Both are very porous, or 'free-draining'. They are, however, usually very thin and look terribly anaemic, and are always in need of a good feed in the form of manure and other organic material. They allow the gardener to grow a wide variety of plants, though not of course acid-loving species such as rhododendrons, ericas and azaleas. Chalk soils are full of life in the form of bacteria, and, although they contain very little plant food, the soil is not only workable during the winter months but will not need liming. The only drawback of chalk and lime soils, notwithstanding a lack of body, is that they can be quite stony, which causes problems for the gardener and farmer alike.

To enrich lime and chalk soils, plenty of organic matter is the order of the day. Keep adding it every autumn, either as a mulch or by digging it in, which will add volume to the soil. The organic matter will also help it to retain moisture, essential during the dry summer months. Adding organic matter will also reduce the alkalinity of chalk soils and increase the range of plants that you can grow successfully.

SANDY SOILS

At first the image conjured up by sandy soil is of a golden beach, but how far from the truth can you get. The type of sand found on the beach is not unrelated to sandy garden soil, but it is golden only because it has very little or no organic matter and because the fragments of rock minerals it contains constantly rub against each other, a process of abrasion which brings forth their natural hue. Sandy soils are usually a light brown in colour, although in some areas where red sandstone is to be found, the soil is a deep burgundy brown. If you rub the soil through your fingers, it will be very gritty and coarse to the touch. Known as 'greedy' and as 'bottomless pits', they have as bad a reputation as clays. Sands are entirely composed of silica, the hardest mineral; unlike clays, they have no base exchanges or colloidal properties and are therefore very inefficient at retaining water or providing plant food. Having depressed you thoroughly about your sandy soils, the good news is that they can be very productive and a joy in the garden when nurtured carefully. Some of the most fertile horticultural and agricultural areas of this country are based on sandy soils.

Sands are known also as 'warm' soils, due to their open construction. Air is allowed to move in them freely, which means that as the temperature warms up in the spring, so does the soil, allowing earlier planting. The beauty of sandy soils is that they can be worked at any time of the year, and they are not alkaline as many people tend to think; on the contrary, many sandy soils are very acidic.

Because of their open nature and texture, rain water is easily leached out through the soil, taking with it the various plant nutrients that may have been introduced in the form of organic matter or fertilizer. However, leaching of the soil really depends on the amount of rainfall. If low, then leaching will be kept to a minimum, and the organic matter in the sand will retain moisture and provide food. If high, then the rainwater will wash out the nutrients and carry away the organic matter. In general, sandy soils are found in the eastern and southern parts of the country, which also happen to have the lowest rainfall, so it's not all bad news. The best remedy for sandy soils is plenty of organic matter, even more than for clay soils. This will retain moisture and provide nutrients, and a dressing of lime will lower the acid content. In some extreme cases, extra fertilizer will be required in order to maintain healthy plant growth. Because they are naturally unrewarding, many areas of sandy soils are left to their own devices, giving us the heaths of Suffolk, Surrey, Norfolk and Dorset. William Cobbett, who I believe gave his name to corn on the cob,

was a traveller, gardener, farmer and writer in the early 1800s. He referred to sandy soils as 'villanous, rascally heaths', and to the benighted people who scratched a living on these sandy tracts of land as heathens. Because of the poor quality and nature of the soil, few people could survive in these areas and they became infamous as highwaymen and robbers. Gad Hill, between Rochester and Gravesend, Finchley Common and Hounslow Heath were all treacherous areas for the traveller, as were many other sandy heaths in this country.

LOAM SOILS

To have a good, loamy soil is really on a par with having heaven on earth. It is the perfect soil type, and people have fought and died for it: the perfect combination of clay, sand and organic matter. Wonderful to work with, productive and full of life, it is every gardener's dream. The clay particles help to conserve water and nutrients, the sand particles allow excess rain water to drain off, and the organic matter which builds up year after year provides a rich tilth for all manner of plants. Some loams do contain more clay than normal and some more sand. Treat these loams as you would treat a heavy clay soil or a light sandy soil: plenty of organic matter will help to build a lovely loam for the future. At one time the traveller could tell when he was passing through a good, loamy district: the fields would be cultivated with all manner of crops, the lanes were narrow in order that the land could be used to its full extent, and elm trees grew tall and strong. There were very few commons to be found, there was little waste land, and there were lots of small, neatly kept villages, for the loam soils provided good profits which were reflected in the state of repair of both houses and farms.

If you have an excess of clay in the loam, then it is advisable to add plenty of organic matter in the autumn months, when the loam is reasonably dry and easy to dig over. The frost will work on the clay with its unique freeze-thaw action, and the organic matter will add body and fibre, opening up the soil. With light, sandy loams, again add plenty of organic matter, digging it in during the autumn and mulching in early spring. You will then have one layer of organic matter deep in the soil and another on the surface which will help to retain moisture. Sandy soils dry out very quickly, and a double helping of organic matter should help solve the moisture problem.

PEAT AND FEN SOILS

In 1662 Sir William Dugdale wrote that the peat lands 'had no element of good. The air cloudy, gross and full of rotten harrs [fogs]. The water putrid and muddy, yea, full of loathsome vermin, the earth spongy and boggy and the fires, noisome, by the stink of smoking hassocks [coarse grass turfs].' Things have changed since his day. The Stuarts started draining the bogs and fens by digging wide ditches into which the water could flow and thence be pumped into the rivers. Today this practice continues but is limited to certain areas, and, although the bogs have changed since the 1600s, you can, if you stand on Langport Hill in Somerset, look out over the flooded land on a cold winter's morning and almost see King Arthur and his men emerging silently from the early morning mists.

Many people tend to think that if you have a peaty soil then you will have no problems whatsoever. No more digging in; no drying out: absolutely wonderful. However, a peaty soil does have its drawbacks. Although it is full of organic matter, a bit like a floating compost heap, it lacks plant food, and it is necessary to add this in the form of fertilizer when growing heavy crops of vegetables, for example. In the ordinary way you may be able to get away without using anything other than a top dressing of manure once a year. As the French agriculturalist Bernard Palissy said in 1563, 'You must admit, that when you bring dung into the field, it is to return to the soil something that has been taken away'. In other words, what we take out of the soil, we must put back in. It only stands to reason. Peaty soils are renowned for being acidic, or sour, and to increase their alkalinity a dressing of lime is a good idea, especially if you intend growing a lot of soft fruit and vegetables, which like a near neutral pH. Test the soil before you add the lime to establish how much is required to raise the pH level. Peaty soils are known for being wet and drainage can be a problem in some areas, but it is the effect of too much drainage that poses more of a problem. Peaty soils are liable to dry out on the surface during hot weather, and should be watered regularly to avoid this. It is difficult to wet the soil thoroughly once it has dried out, and it will not retain the moisture as it did before, with the result that plant growth and health are affected. You have probably noticed this when using peat-based composts. Two successful crops grown on peaty or fen soils are celery and mustard; the latter has helped to bring fame and wealth to Norwich in Norfolk.

You might have thought the end of this chapter on soils was in sight by now, but before we leave the subject, there are several things still to be covered. Everyone takes it for granted that the soil is just a mixture of minerals and organic matter. But what about the creatures living in the soil that act as 'go-betweens', ensuring that the plants we put in our gardens get the most out of the soil? In every handful of soil is not only a piece of history but millions of bacteria, fungi, algae and probably the odd earthworm to boot. Before you throw down the handful in disgust and reach for the rubber gloves, there isn't much in it that is going to harm you personally. For a start, most of the organisms mentioned cannot be seen by the human eye without using a very powerful microscope. You can divide these soil organisms into several different groups: fungi, bacteria, actinomycetes, algae, lichens, protozoa, rhizopods and phages. Haven't they got wonderful names?

Let's start with fungi. Mushrooms and toadstools and the like spring immediately to mind. Well, these are fungi and they do thrive upon decomposed material, but there are many other types of fungi that cannot be seen by the naked eye which are both beneficial and damaging to soil and plants alike. In just one gram of soil there are reputed to be over a million fungi. Although they are a form of plant, they do not contain chlorophyll, which gives the plants their green colouring. Many fungi are parasitic, living upon healthy plant tissue and causing disease, which may appear as mildew, rust or black spot. Saprophytes are fungi that benefit the soil by feeding upon the organic matter, breaking it down and preparing it for bacteria, which will work on it still further, although in exceptionally acid soils it is the fungi that are responsible for breaking down the organic matter into humus. In a compost heap, especially mine, fungi form a white layer near the top of the pile, where there is plenty of moisture and heat. Fungi will produce ammonia in the compost heap, but unfortunately they are not capable of nitryfying it. All fungi start off as spores and go on to produce a clear or opaque stem called a hypha, which then enlarges to become a mycelium, the vegetative body of a fungus. From the mycelium enzymes are produced which attack organic matter in order to obtain food. Eventually the mycelium will produce a head in which spores develop that will later be dispersed. One type of fungi we all come into contact with (at least I do quite frequently) is that on bread. The white, fluffy stuff is the mycelium and the black pinheads that eventually appear, if you keep the bread long enough, are the spores. Mycorrhiza are fungi found around the roots of plants. These are specialized in their activities and in many cases cannot survive without the association of living plants, which produce food for them from organic matter. While they are alive, protein and carbohydrate (nitrogen and other nutrients), are stored in the mycelium; when they die they are attacked by bacteria, which release the nitrogen, converting it into nitrate. In many heath and woodland situations mycorrhiza are essential for tree and plant growth as the soil is usually very impoverished. Mycorrhizal activity also induces disease resistance in plants.

The word bacteria brings to mind those television adverts that have you running round like a headless chicken, squirting bleach down your sinks, drains and toilets and anywhere else you can think of to kill the little blighters. For if you don't, the end will be nigh. These wonderful single-cell organisms are on average only one thousandth of a millimetre in size. We all tend to think of them as being harmful, but if it wasn't for some types of bacteria, many of us wouldn't be here today. Without bacteria in the soil, we would be in a very sorry state indeed, for they have an important part to play in the life of the soil, of plants and of people too. The most important type of bacteria, comprising a few humble species, is responsible for nitrogen fixation upon which human, animal and plant life depends: a sobering thought indeed. Now, as I have mentioned, plant, animal and human life all contain protein. The waste products, or remains, of plants and animals are broken down by bacteria into humus. This gives off ammonia, which is oxidized by bacteria known as nitrosomonas to produce nitrites. (These are poisonous to plants, but the process takes place so quickly that the plant is not affected.) The nitrites are then oxidized by bacteria called nitrobacter to form nitrates. The plants absorb the nitrate

The nitrogen cycle: ammonia and nitrogen given off by decomposition are converted into nitrates producing protein for animal and plant life.

and convert it into protein which is then eaten by animals, their waste or remains is spread on the land and the cycle starts all over again. If the land is bare of plants and there is nothing to absorb the nitrate, then it will be leached out by the rain into watercourses, drainage ditches etc. The process just described is known as nitrification, part of the nitrogen cycle, and in the diagram opposite you will see exactly how it works.

Without nitrates in the soil, many plants, especially cereals and root crops, upon which we are dependent, would be unable to grow. A few grasses and the odd bog plant might survive, and in tropical climates rice would be the only crop. We wouldn't even have our gardens.

Nitrification will only take place in warm soils, and is most effective in limed or chalky soils. In very acid soils, where there is no lime, plants are forced to use ammonia as a source of nitrogen. On soils that are heavy and wet for long periods of time a process called denitrification can take place. This is the reverse of nitrification: the nitrates are converted into nitrites and thence into nitrogen gas which escapes into the atmosphere. Bacteria known as azotobacter and clostridium convert the nitrogen gas in the air back into nitrates. Thunderstorms, helped by the oxygen in the air, are also capable of turning the nitrogen gas into nitrates which are dissolved in the rain.

I expect you have often heard people say that they are planting a crop of peas, clover or even lupins as they are nitrogen-fixing plants. What they mean is that these plants, and others from the legume family, have nodules on their roots which contain bacteria called *Rhizobium leguminosarum*. These bacteria are capable of absorbing nitrogen from the air and converting it into nitrates as food for the plant. But this will only happen if the bacteria are well supplied with calcium, phosphate and other trace elements, hence the need to ensure that your soil is well limed if acidic, and that it is given plenty of compost. In return the plant will supply the bacteria with food in the form of carbohydrate. However, if there is plenty of nitrate or ammonia available in the soil, the nitrogen-fixing bacteria will fix more nitrogen than can be absorbed by the plant. When the plant dies this surplus nitrogen is released to enrich the soil, especially if the dead plant is used as a green manure and dug in. It would appear, however, that each type of nitrogen-fixing plant has a bacteria which is peculiar to that plant alone. Bacteria found in the nodules of legumes, for example, will not be of benefit to lupins and vice versa, especially if lupins have not been grown on that piece of land before. A crop that is finding favour with farmers today is lucerne. Unfortunately, it is not indigenous to Great Britain and its seed often has to be inoculated with its appropriate bacteria in order to obtain a strong and healthy crop and to ensure that the crop sown afterwards can benefit from a nitrogen-enriched soil.

Many bacteria are very beneficial to the soil. Some can break down chemical compounds, others act upon mineral matter, releasing plant food into the soil, and some are adept at overpowering chemicals added to the soil, such as insecticides. In fact biochemical companies today can produce bacteria to overcome many problems, not only in the medical field but also in everyday life. Britain's coastal areas are vulnerable to oil pollution, and bacteria have now been indentified that can ingest the hydrocarbons in the oil and reduce their pollutant effects.

So look after and encourage the bacteria in your gardens by ensuring that the soil is kept 'open' and moist, enrich it with compost and, should it be very acidic, a dressing of lime would not go amiss, though always do a soil test with litmus paper or a specialist soil-testing kit beforehand just to make sure that everything is tickety-boo.

Actinomycetes are supposedly a cross between, or a hybrid form of, bacteria and fungi, although no one as yet is quite sure. These organisms, which resemble fungi, are said to be responsible for giving us that heavenly smell that lingers in the air when rain has fallen on a summer's day. This earthy, invigorating odour is said to be caused by the dampness of the spores of the actinomycetes that are released into the air after rain. Well, that's one theory and there are probably a thousand others, but this one does stand to reason. Some actinomycetes, although resembling fungi with their mycelial threads and spores, act like bacteria, needing aerobic conditions and feeding upon decomposed material. One well-known species of actinomycetes is streptomyces, which is used in the production of antibiotics. Others are known to be parasitic on plants; one such is commonly known as potato scab.

We've all seen it. We've all touched it. Ughh! It's enough to send shivers down your spine: that horrible green, slimy stuff that grows on rocks, stones and bare soil and creeps up the panes of glass in the greenhouse. But how you pronounce it is another matter. Is it with a hard 'g' or a soft one; is it al-gee or al-gay? The argument is never ending. Anyway, algae, however you say it, contains chlorophyll. It is this that gives it its green colouring and enables it to absorb carbon dioxide which, when combined with water, forms sugars and other carbohydrates by means of energy from the sun in the process known as photosynthesis. Different algae are found in different situations, some in the soil, some in ponds and some in the sea. What function they actually play is not fully understood, but there is one type of algae that fixes nitrogen from the soil (in a similar way as do the azotobacter) to provide protein. Green algae grow on acid soils, but in the Orient a blue-green algae known as nostocs, which can be found on neutral and fertile soils, grow in vast numbers on the surface of the bog-like paddy fields. Here the algae provide oxygen for the roots of the rice plants, together with nitrogen which has been fixed from the air. Algae are usually covered with a thin film of moisture, hence their sliminess.

Very often lichens (pronounced litchins, lytchens, lyshens or likens – take your pick) are confused with mosses. Lichens are those flat, grey and yellow growths that you see on stones, roof tiles, trees, stone tubs and garden ornaments, and they consist of a combination of algae and certain types of fungi. Lichens were probably the very first plant colonizers. The fungi would fix itself on a rock, for example, providing a firm base for the lichen, whose rough surface catches dust particles; when the lichen dies the organic matter left behind forms a basis on which mosses can grow, and, as time progresses and organic matter is built up, larger plants take hold.

Five times larger than bacteria, protozoa are microscopic animals that devour both good and bad bacteria. There are two types of protozoa to be found in the soil, namely flagellates and amoeba. Flagellates have one or more tails to help them move around, some feed on organic matter and one species is green in colour. Amoeba are larger than flagellates and their protoplasm, which changes shape, helps them to move around. They prey upon bacteria, which they surround with their protoplasm and then ingest. Other protozoa, algae and even yeasts are devoured by them, and one type of amoeba feeds upon the potato eelworm which causes so much damage to potato crops.

Other micro-predators in the soil include rhizopods, which – though mainly found in arable land – will also feed upon potato eelworm, and acrasieae which feed upon bacteria in a similar fashion to that of the amoeba. Phages are viruses that destroy bacteria, although only certain types of phage will attack certain bacteria.

In addition to the soil organisms, many other organisms exist that have an effect on the soil. Eelworms, as mentioned, are tiny, transparent worms less than 1mm in length. Some, like the potato eelworm, attack plants, causing damage and disease; others will quite happily feed upon the organic matter in the soil. Insects, ants, beetles and worms all have an effect upon the soil, by ingesting decayed material or preying upon soil organisms. Earthworms must be the most famous of these soil improvers and dwellers, but a whole chapter ('The Early Compost Maker Catches the Worm') has been devoted to this marvellous little fellow later on.

CHAPTER THREE

COMPOSTING YOUR WAY TO HEALTH

And down in lovely muck I've lain,
Happy till I woke again

A.E. HOUSEMAN (1859–1936)

Did you know that there are almost as many ways of making compost as there are Heinz varieties? I've actually met a married couple who have tried almost every composting process known to man, and still, after thirty years, they have not managed to produce that wonderful dark, cool, almost seductive material known as humus.

Compost is not a new invention. For centuries peoples throughout the world have recognized the fact that the land needs feeding, and that there are magical ingredients in the soil that will produce healthy and bountiful crops year in and year out. People in the land of Mesopotamia (now known as Iraq), between the rivers Euphrates and Tigris, would ensure that these rivers flooded their land every spring for they had seen the effect on their crops of the silt left behind when the water receded. According to records dating from around 2000 BC, the Mesopotamians were the instigators of modern Arabic farming techniques, for the flooding of plains by these rivers and many others throughout the Middle East is still common practice today.

In the twelfth century there lived in Seville a Moor called Ibn-al-Awam who was fascinated by the effects that certain waste materials had on the growth of plants. He wrote a book about agriculture in which he described the various practices carried out by the people of the Middle East that had been handed down through time. In this book is a detailed account of how compost should be made, Middle Eastern fashion.

A pit was dug in the ground in which all dungs were placed: human excrement, dove droppings from the dovecotes, asses and cow manure. Then powdered earth was added but this had to come from the bottom of a previous pit or manure heap. Then blood was introduced in large quantities. Human blood was considered an excellent component, but if it was not available, then camel's or sheep's blood would have to suffice. Water was added and all the ingredients mixed thoroughly; rain apparently activated decomposition in the pit. The mixture was left to its own devices until it had turned black, when it was dried under cover, mixed with more powdered earth and spread around the garden.

There is no doubt that some of the most beautiful gardens in the world are to be found where the Arabs and Moors settled and developed their culture. Before you think of following Ibn-al-Awam's recipe, I am afraid to say that one or two of the above ingredients are not readily available in this country, namely human blood and camel's blood. Although of course, you might know differently.

Until the early part of this century there was really only one way to manage your compost heap, especially if you wanted good quality compost for your hotbeds and mushrooms, and that was to aerate or turn your compost on a regular basis. In the early days the compost heap contained a wide variety of ingredients, not just the waste vegetable or plant matter that we use today. Many people kept a few chickens, the odd house cow, horses and ponies, pigeons and even a pig (though I don't for one minute suggest that you rush out and acquire one of these 'live activators'). The compost heap was usually quite near the house and adjacent to the buildings where animals or birds were kept. The vegetable waste and leftover food from the kitchen was fed to the chickens or pig, they in turn ingested this material, and their waste was added to the compost heap, where it was broken down by bacteria. By this means a ready supply of compost was made available to fertilize the garden. If you didn't have an inside lavatory in those days, you often had to use a privy housed in an old wooden shed at the bottom of the garden, and the contents of this were added to the compost heap as well. In some places where they didn't have a loo, you'd have to use the dungheap. I'm glad to say that we've come a long way since then.

The message that I am trying to get over is that today we expect to create wonderful material from our compost heaps but we only put in material of a low food value, such as ordinary kitchen or garden waste, which has not been through a live activator. How can we hope to get the old-fashioned type of compost if we put nothing of any worth into our compost heaps in the first place? You just can't beat a bit of manure in any shape or form if you want a head start in producing good compost. The reason why my

heap is so successful (says she proudly) is because it combines plenty of waste from the cows, which is high in protein to produce bacteria, lots of moisture and plenty of air through turning. Not only that, but my heaps are a decent size. I'm not suggesting that you create a compost heap twenty feet (6m) long, ten feet (3m) wide and four feet (1.2m) high; you should get good results from a heap or bin four feet (1.2m) square, which will contain at least a ton of material. This may sound a lot but you'll be surprised at how quickly a bin four feet (1.2m) square fills up. It will generate plenty of heat if you turn it once a fortnight, although every seven days is better. If this all sounds like too much hard work, well you could be right, although when I first started composting, I did it all by hand. Aeration is one of the most important factors in any composting process. Unfortunately, with the hectic lives we lead today, not many of us have either the time or the energy to adhere to the hard and fast rule of aeration before addition: always turn or aerate the top eight to ten inches (20–25cm) of the heap before you add any more material to it.

First of all, however, let's get the terminology right. The waste material that we form into a pile is known as organic matter, the definition of organic being something that was once living and is now dead, completing the cycle of life. It has absolutely nothing whatsoever to do with the chemicals or pesticides you have sprayed around the garden. But the term is widely applied today to food products grown without the use of chemical sprays or artificial fertilizers, with the result that a lot of people are confused, especially me. Surely a better word can be found to define the principles of cultivation that have been with us for a few hundred years. I can't say since time immemorial as we didn't start gardening or farming 'professionally' until the late 1500s, and gardening didn't really take off until the early 1800s when the Georgian gardeners and farmers became more adventurous and knowledgeable, mainly as a result of learning from their own mistakes. They even used artificial manures then. The trouble is that the word organic means so many things to so many people, and what other word can one use? Another terminological muddle relates to compost and humus. Once organic material is put in a heap the composting process begins, and at this point the material is undoubtedly compost. After the composting process has finished, however, and the organic material has broken down, the end product is, strictly speaking, humus. In fact we all seem to refer to it as compost, whether taken before completion of decomposition or after. But let's not get too technical, I'm quite happy calling it compost and have done so for many years. The most important thing is that someone somewhere has at long last been encouraging people to make their own compost, and to put natural waste matter back into the soil where it belongs. This is absolutely crucial. As I explained in Chapter Two, the earth needs replenishing with vital humic material if it is to perform successfully the arduous tasks that we ask of it.

With smaller gardens there is less room for a compost heap, and most people chuck household waste in the bin and that's the end of it. They then spend a small fortune on peat to bulk up their garden soil, add a few proprietary fertilizers, and only when the garden really begins to look sick do they decide to give it some proper nourishment. In most cases, unfortunately, even where people do have compost heaps or bins, they have been unsuccessful in producing compost that looks sufficiently wholesome and agreeable to spread around their gardens.

COMPOSTING CONUNDRUMS

What actually happens in your compost heap? If you were able to shrink to the size of a fly and wander around a compost heap, it would be like walking round an extremely busy hotel kitchen on an exceptionally hot day. The food is delivered to the kitchen in its raw state, various sous chefs work on it, chopping, grating, beating and kneading it before mixing all the ingredients together; the master chefs then cook these ingredients with the aid of heat and water, and finally a waiter takes the finished dish to the waiting customer, where it arrives cooked to perfection and ready to eat. The compost heap works in exactly the same manner. Organic material is broken down by bacteria, micro-organisms and the effects of air and water. As the bacteria work away, their energy is released in the form of heat, and as they multiply in the favourable conditions they eventually run out of food and die. The increasing heat of the compost heap encourages the growth of toadstools and other fungi, sometimes seen on the heap, and activates the spread of more bacteria and micro-organisms such as actinomycetes. Then when the temperature has peaked, and all available food has been ingested, the heat of the compost heap falls slowly to the ambient temperature, allowing soil fauna into the heap. They forage around on the micro-organisms left behind, both living and dead (the dead organisms forming humic acids) and, after leaving the heap to mature for several months, you are left with a wonderful pile of humus. Nothing mysterious about composting at all. No witch-craft, potions or magic spells, just Mother Nature doing what comes naturally.

LADY MUCK'S GUIDE TO COMPOSTING

There are no hard and fast rules for composting; all I can give you are guidelines to help you produce wonderful compost for your garden. First of all, you have to remember that making compost is a bit like making a Christmas pudding: the richness of the ingredients, the care you take in making it and the time it is left to mature are all important factors in achieving a good end product. If stirring with a spoon is replaced by aerating with a fork, you are almost there. It will take several months, if not a year or so, to make compost, though you can speed up the process by ensuring that all materials are crushed before being added to the heap. Cabbage stems can be trampled underfoot and large, leafy material shredded into smaller pieces. Excess moisture from leaves can cause unnecessary problems, and green, leafy material should be allowed to wilt for a couple of days before being added to the heap as this will ensure that the material dries out a little and loses as much moisture as it can.

If you are keen to shorten the composting process, I recommend the use of a shredder, which saves a lot of time and gives a consistent end result. And if you throw in some manure, then you will get wonderful compost in double-quick time: there is a lot to be said for the magic of muck. Shredders are quite expensive, however, and are not essential unless you are determined to really go for it and get composting in earnest. I must stop saying this for I always remember a joke about two earthworms in a graveyard, one of whom was composting in Ernest. Hiring a shredder for a morning is a lot cheaper than buying one, or you could perhaps get together with some composting friends and share a shredder for a day. If you look through the For Sale columns in your local newspaper, you will often see shredders for sale at quite competitive prices, but make sure that the metal teeth are undamaged and that the shredder in general is in good working order, and ask to see it working before you buy. If you don't want to be bothered with a shredder, just ensure that the material you put on your compost heap is broken down first into small pieces, either tearing it apart with your hands or chopping it up with the garden shears; it all helps. Don't put more than twenty per cent of your lawn clippings or a lot of paper on your main compost heap; quite frankly, you're better off taking the clippings down to the recycling tip and the paper to a special collection point. The trouble with newspapers and grass clippings is that they decompose into a horrible wet mess, blocking out the air and causing the compost to turn stale. If you're reluctant to part with your lawn clippings, keep them in a separate heap as they break down very quickly, having been chopped into little pieces by the lawn mower and aerated as they are collected. After four months they should provide suitable material to use as a mulch around the garden, but remember, there isn't much food value in lawn clippings unless they are from young spring grass, so don't rely on them to feed your plants; mix them in with other composted material which will provide the necessary plant food and allow the lawn clippings to help to retain moisture.

You should not have any need for an activator such as sulphate of ammonia or quicklime unless you are putting a lot of woody material on your heap. Woody material contains a high amount of carbon, which will leach nitrogen out of your compost heap to break itself down. One reason why I don't like using straw is that it has a high carbon to nitrogen ratio, and many farmers are having problems with their arable ground now that straw and stubble burning has been banned. The straw uses all the nitrogen in the soil to break itself down, taking anything up to a year to do so. It then releases the nitrogen very slowly, but too late for next year's crop. You then feed the soil with artificial nitrate, which is absorbed by the straw, with the result that double the amount of nitrogen is given off when it has fully decomposed and your crop suddenly bolts, weakening the plant.

One way of accelerating the activity in your heap is to aerate on a regular basis, and it doesn't cost you a penny to do it. I like to see a compost heap placed directly on the ground as this enables worms to get into it and help to aerate and break down the compost further. The ground also acts as insulation and allows for drainage. Do not put your compost heap in the wettest part of the garden or in a hollow, where water will have difficulty in draining away and your heap will become stagnant and foul smelling. Allow the heap some access to sunshine. Although many people say that this is unnecessary, the sun will help to heat up the compost and keep it warm. Keep the heap covered at all times; this helps to retain moisture and, if you want to encourage worms into your compost, they will work better in the dark anyway. Use a material such as old carpet or sacking which has the power to absorb moisture or release it as required. I don't like polythene as it doesn't allow the heap to breathe. If you find that your heap is drying out, don't throw your washing-up water on it in the hopes that this will re-activate it. Water should be added gradually so that the material can absorb it but does not become dripping wet.

One rule which must be stringently observed is never add diseased material to the heap, for example plants or cuttings affected with rust or mildew or, perish the thought, wood infected with honey fungus. These diseases will incubate in the heap, which provides them with an ideal breeding ground, and if you spread contaminated compost around the garden you will be in big trouble. Nor should you add left-over meat to the heap; this only attracts vermin such as foxes, rats and mice which could carry diseases from other compost heaps in which they have been scavenging. Not only that, but they will make a hell of a mess of your heap, throwing material around while foraging for that elusive morsel.

Weeds should be left out of a compost heap if they are in flower and never, never, never, put them in if they are in seed. Some weeds can be beneficial to the heap if they are young, nettles being a firm favourite with some gardeners as they produce a lot of potash. Let the saying 'One year's seeds, seven years of weeds' be a warning to you. Either burn the offending weeds or take them to the council tip, together with any diseased material that you may have in the garden. Please remember that it is unlawful to have a bonfire on a

Sunday, and always make sure that the wind blowing the smoke from your bonfire will not offend your neighbours. There's nothing worse than smoke-dried washing; I speak from experience. The ashes from the bonfire will be full of potash so don't waste them; mix them in with the compost or spread them around the garden. If you are using wood to make a compost bin, do not treat it prior to use as the chemicals can get into the compost. A coating of creosote is a good idea (and I just love the smell) though it seems to kill everything in sight, and you do have to be careful with it because it is very caustic. If using second-hand timber, check for disease such as honey fungus. You'll see the caramel-coloured fungus growing on it if it is infected, but by this stage the wood won't be fit for much anyway. Don't panic if you get the ordinary umbrella toadstools on your compost; this is a good sign that the material has heated up well. You won't get toadstools in the garden when you spread the compost as the fungi responsible need a lot of heat in order to grow. If there are no worms in your compost, don't worry. They don't like hot compost and will only enter the heap when it has decomposed well and the heat has gone. You should find them around the bottom of the compost heap; look out for their casts. You will also find lots of other insects, such as woodlice, centipedes and springtails in the compost. These creatures thrive on the organic matter in the heap and, I am afraid to say, you won't be able to keep them out. If the compost is good enough for them, it's certainly good enough for the garden. With a wooden bin you'll get rather more woodlice than normal. If you want to add lime to the compost heap, always check the pH before you spread it around the garden, as plants such as rhododendrons, azaleas and camellias are not too fond of lime. In a chalky or limestone area, you should find that you don't need to add lime to the compost heap; it's there already in the plants. The composting process takes less time in the summer, when the air is warm and conditions more favourable in general, than in the winter. Keep your compost heap warm in winter by insulating it well with old carpet or sacking, and don't turn it so often: once every three to four weeks is enough. When the heap is full you should only turn the top over three or four times, then leave it well covered and allow it to mature for two months. During this time it won't hurt to check the contents just to ensure that everything is going well, and to make any adjustments required.

One last point about compost ingredients is that if you add

material from a very poor soil to the compost heap, you must realize that, although it will contain essential minerals, it may be somewhat lacking in nutrients. A compost heap needs a high protein feed with lots of nitrogen, so if you know that your soil is poor and your plants have little to offer in this department it would be worth your while to add some animal manure, sulphate of ammonia, Growmore, dried blood or hoof and horn. I find that most gardeners have one or all of the latter ingredients lurking in their wooden garden temples. This problem of poor nutrient compost occurs quite often in neglected gardens but is soon remedied by the addition of a little tonic to the compost heap.

Many people recommend building a compost heap in layers, alternating layers of grass clippings and leafy, shrubby material, separated by a layer of soil. The nitrogen-fixing bacteria in the soil absorbs the ammonia gas given off by the compost, enhancing the fertility value of the heap. Unfortunately, if the compost is not hot enough to sterilize the weed seeds contained in the soil, the nitrogen fixed by the bacteria will be used by the weeds for growth. If you wish to add material to your compost heap in layers, then may I suggest that you use a layer of either sphagnum moss peat or coir. These will soak up excess moisture, although the latter is not a substrate and does not contain the essential bacteria for fixing nitrogen. Do not use sedge peat as this substrate is ineffectual in a compost heap.

Other people recommend that compost be compressed by either jumping up and down on it or continually striking it with the back of a shovel. This knocks all the air out of the heap and the compost will take about eighteen months to break down. Compaction of the compost heap is a little like making silage on the farm; the grass is compressed and air extracted to preserve the heap before covering it with polythene. Although slight decomposition will occur, the end product contains essential energy. If air is allowed into the silage heap, the grass will decompose and become mouldy as the moisture cannot escape through the polythene, and we will lose vital winter feed for our cows.

The rest of this chapter covers several different methods of composting to show you what can be done in gardens of various sizes, using materials and composting systems that are widely available. All these methods have been tried and tested and have worked for the people involved, but ultimately it depends on you, on how much time and effort you want to give to composting and, more importantly, on how much fun you want to have, as to which method you choose. Composting is great fun: you can make a wonderful outdoor kitchen, cheap and easy to run, and there's nothing like talking about the subject over dinner. Well, they say you must never talk about politics, religion or sex, so all that's left to me is composting. It's amazing what you learn.

THE S.A.I.F. COMPOST BIN

S.A.I.F. stands for Stan and Ivy Formula, in honour of two of my composting friends. I was asked to appear on a TV gardening programme based in Southampton to help solve a compost problem for a well-known writer. Unfortunately, the writer was unable to appear and a replacement had to be found. The production team then rang me to ask if I knew of anyone living in Dorset who had a problem with their compost heap. It was a bit like being asked if you knew anyone living on the moon. It just so happened that I was giving a talk at the Dorset Federation of Women's Institutes and Markets AGM the following day, and told the TV director that I would see what I could do. Having given my talk, everyone was laughing and there was a good, appreciative buzz in the air, so I asked the audience, who packed the hall like a wall-to-wall carpet, whether anyone had a problem with their compost heap. Immediately a woman shot out of her seat, arms waving in the air, shouting 'Yes, we do! We do!' 'Well,' I said, 'aren't you the lucky ones, because you are now going to be on television!' At this the woman looked a little shocked, the hall rang with laughter and cries of 'Autograph! Autograph!' filled the air. To cut a long story short, this lovely couple called Stan and Ivy had been trying to make compost for over thirty years. Not a morsel of kitchen waste had ever seen the dustbin, and, having read every book they could lay their hands on and having tried every technique, they were now having problems with their present system.

On the day of filming, I arrived at their house early and went into the garden with Stan and Ivy to see for myself where they were going wrong. The camera crew didn't turn up for forty-five minutes, so we had an enthusiastic chat about compost and what could be done about the situation. The main problem was their compost bins – two blue plastic drums twenty-four inches (60cm) wide and about three feet (90cm) deep. They had been raised slightly off the ground, their bottoms had been cut off and replaced with mesh and their tops had been cut to make lids. Polythene

covers served to stop excess water getting in. These bins were in the dingiest, darkest place in the garden, under pine trees and behind a fence. Poor old compost. Stan and Ivy had been a little embarrassed about the rotten, foul-smelling stuff they had had in their bins before I arrived and had emptied most of it out, leaving a small amount in the bottom. It didn't look too bad, very anaerobic and wet, but it had toadstools on the top and worms in the bottom, so things weren't too disastrous. When the camera crew turned up they had a look at the bins, told me not to touch the toadstools as they would make a wonderful shot, and then spent quite a bit of time filming Stan and Ivy as they recounted their problems over the years. All they wanted was a lovely, steaming heap of compost and some dark, crumbly material at the end. Unfortunately, with their system it was very unlikely that this would happen. To get organic material to heat up you do need volume. Compost heaps should be placed on the ground and should be at least three feet (90cm) wide and three feet (90cm) deep, preferably four feet by four feet (1.2m by 1.2m). This creates wonderful insulation and generates terrific heat, and sets you well on the way to making good compost. Today, with our small gardens, we don't have room to spare for a heap as large as this, and we like things to look tidy, hence the rush for 'dalek' compost systems. I suppose a sprawling compost heap is not a pretty sight, but if it works who cares?

Anyway, after Stan and Ivy had finished their story, it was my turn. Now, I had thought this would be a straightforward presentation. You know the sort of thing: you charge in there, tell them where they've gone wrong, show them what to do, have a sample of the end product, giving them an idea of what to aim for, generally act like a whirlwind and then, much to their relief, disappear out of their lives for ever. How could I be so wrong? I was expected to act. My local pantomime group would have been proud of me, but all I wanted to do was go home. I couldn't believe what the crew were asking of me. I had to jump out from behind trees, garden fork in hand, hold the frame for ten while they inserted a flash of lightning, then tell Stan and Ivy that I would remedy their problem immediately. No script, no autocue. What should I say? Come on Jane, I thought, think of something, and pretty quick too. The only thing I could come up with were the lines, 'Never fear, Lady Muck is here, and I'll guarantee you compost within the year'.

I then got told off for making it rhyme, and was instructed to run behind the wooden fence, throw the bin lids about and generally wreak havoc with their foul compost. What I forgot, in my frenzied outburst of acting, were the poor old toadstools. I completely mashed them to bits. But it's amazing what you can do with a few bits of sellotape, and in no time we had the toadstools back in the act again. We seemed to spend an awful lot of time filming without really getting over anything constructive about the composting, but my moment of glory was coming. And it literally was just a moment. Poor old Stan and I had to cart one of his heavy bins of compost onto his lawn, and then at long last I got my chance to tell Stan and Ivy how to solve their problem. The director asked me how long it would take for me to go through the actions of composting. 'At least an hour and a half', I said very precisely. 'You haven't got an hour and a half' came the retort; 'this is only a half an hour programme'. 'Oh well,' I said, 'what about ten minutes? I should be able to do it in that time.' 'You have got one minute exactly', replied the director. I was dumbfounded. My description must have come over a bit like a Pinky and Perky routine. I don't think I have ever crammed so many words into such a short space of time in all my life, and I felt sorry for the viewers. It didn't really give them much of an idea about composting, and the director admitted that there was more to it than meets the eye.

Stan and Ivy have since moved their compost bins to a nice little spot beside the garden shed, where the bins will get sunshine and plenty of air. They still wanted to keep the mesh in the bottom, but the bins are now raised off the ground on bricks. A plastic tub has been inserted underneath, where the liquid produced from the composting can be caught and used in the greenhouse. They now turn the top layer of compost before they add any more material and already things are looking promising. In fact, one bin has been left to carry on composting and they have started on the second. I suggested that when the first had been composting for a couple of months, but was still being turned occasionally, they empty out the contents and leave it under cover to dry out for a month or so. This is what I used to do with my worm compost (see Chapter Four). Although very humic, it was wet, and, if you wanted to use it for potting, it helped to spread it out on the floor of the shed and scrape off the layers as they dried out, putting this material in old compost or fertilizer sacks. Remember, the compost has been outside in all the elements and can be a lot wetter than you think.

THE LORD LUVADUCK METHOD

I have a friend who calls himself Lord Luvaduck. Having tried unsuccessfully to make compost in a three-feet (90-cm) square bin, he decided to line the sides with black plastic sheeting and to raise the bottom slightly off the ground to allow for circulation of air. He then made himself another bin, very much like the New Zealand type, a slatted wooden box, and bought himself a small shredder. Instead of simply turning the compost from bin to bin once a fortnight, he now puts it all through the shredder each time. The last time I went to see him I took him some fresh cow manure, and this was added to the compost at a ratio of twenty-five per cent to one barrow load of waste material. The heat generated was fantastic, the compost was coming along nicely and, because everything had been broken down into bite-size pieces by the shredder, the bacteria were able to move in and start ingesting all the quicker. Lord Luvaduck's recipe has certainly worked, but although he has an average-size garden he does, unfortunately for him but fortunately for me, have to buy in compost to supplement his own. His two compost bins are in an area where air can circulate and

there is plenty of natural light and sunshine, and the results are a credit to him. You wouldn't know what was going on in these boxes unless you took off the old matting on top and delved in underneath.

The biggest problem that I encounter is what to do with lawn clippings. Grass is a notorious element in the compost heap. Admittedly, it heats up beautifully, but I would treat it as a separate entity altogether and only put a few handfuls in your main compost heap. Lord Luvaduck takes his grass clippings down to the local tip, where they are recycled, and uses only a couple of handfuls in the compost heap. As he pointed out to me, grass clippings are ideal as a mulch but for making good compost you don't really need them. If you don't want to give over your precious compost bin to grass clippings, then one way of composting them successfully is to put them in bin bags, with small pin pricks in, and leave them for six weeks, turning the bags over once a week. Friends of mine do this on a regular basis and use the end product as a mulch to hold moisture in the ground. The clippings should not smell but, if your lawn is full of weeds, think twice before placing this material anywhere on the garden. And do ensure that, if you treat your lawn with hormone weed-killers or other chemicals, you do not put grass cuttings on the compost heap as this will seriously affect the compost and, in the long run, the plants around which you place it.

Lord Luvaduck's nephew, who gardens on a free-draining soil which I presume is very sandy, has come up with a novel idea. He digs a series of pits in the ground and throws into them all his lawn clippings. After a year these pits are full of wonderfully dark humic material which he uses in large quantities as a mulch around the garden, and very effective it is too. On the sandy soil the moisture given off from the decomposition of the lawn clippings is allowed to drain away freely, and the soil itself acts as insulation, keeping the heat in and encouraging the bacteria to ingest the material. Moisture is allowed in through a covering of old carpet. The only drawback to compost in pits is that it can be a little difficult to get out.

THE MUSCLE-BUILDING COMPOST HEAP

This system is so called because it consists of three bins which have to be turned on a regular basis, moving material from A to B to C, keeping you fit as well as producing wonderful material. It works like this. You put fresh waste in bin A, and when this is full you take the bottom half of the material and place it in bin B. When bin B is full you take material from the bottom half and place it in bin C, adding more from bin B at monthly intervals. By the time bin C is full the material from the bottom half will be excellent compost and can be placed around the garden – if, that is, by this time you haven't done your back in. This system is very hard work and, quite frankly, I'm not sure it's really worth it. An easier option is to have three compost bins on the go, to turn the material over before adding any fresh matter and, when you have a full bin, just to leave it for another six months to compost thoroughly. It saves any back-breaking work and the results are more or less as good. The purpose of moving it is really to aerate it, and you might as well do that as you are filling it up. The same system can be practised with two bins, but you might find that you fill them so quickly that, to make room for more waste, you start using the material before it has thoroughly composted, in which case you will not get the full benefit from it.

COMMERCIAL COMPOST BINS

The market now seems to be flooded with plastic dalek-type compost bins, each and every one promising ready-made compost at the bat of an eyelid. Depending on what you put into these bins and where you place them, you can get good compost within three to four months, especially if you fill the bin in one go with a mixture of material, throw in some sulphate of ammonia for good measure and leave it for at least three months. Some people have had wonderful results, others not so: the quality of the material and the siting of the bin make all the difference. Look for a sturdy, heavy compost bin (light ones blow around if you haven't got much material in them) and buy the largest you can. Small bins are ideal for very small gardens but the bigger the bin the more effective the heat will be, the quicker the breakdown of material and the better the compost at the end. The only trouble with big bins is that it can be a bit of a pain getting compost out from the bottom. Some of them are also extremely expensive and, although they keep everything tidy, an ordinary compost heap is cheaper and may be more effective. Some people go to extreme lengths to hide the fact that they have compost bins in the garden, even making them out of wood to resemble bee hives or dog kennels, or decorating them with window boxes full of flowers. Others hide their bins behind trelliswork covered with clematis, roses and even runner beans, which seem to do exceptionally well next to all that organic material.

If you are wondering why I haven't so far made more than a passing mention of worms and their involvement in composting, its because I felt these little creatures deserved a section of their own and have therefore devoted the following chapter to them.

CHAPTER FOUR

THE EARLY COMPOST MAKER CATCHES THE WORM

I would not enter on my list of friends
(Tho grac'd with polish'd names and
fine sense yet wanting sensibility)
The man who needlessly sets foot upon a worm!

WILLIAM COWPER (1731–1800)

My passion for worms was ignited by my father back in the early 1980s. With the introduction of milk quotas on dairy farms in 1984, many farmers found that they had to diversify in order to maintain their farm incomes if they wanted to survive. A lot of farmers ventured into very unusual practices, such as milking goats or sheep, ice-cream making, yoghurt making, B & B, even the rearing of llamas, angora goats and ostriches. My father went in for worms.

Having seen an advertisement in *Farmers Weekly*, telling him how he could make a £100 a ton from his farmyard manure (FYM), father decided to investigate a little further and found that, if you fed this material to certain types of worm, they would ingest it and the casts they excreted would form the basis of a garden compost. It was said to be a profitable enterprise that required very little capital input. It sounded absolutely wonderful – the answer to a lot of farmers' prayers, especially here in the West Country where we can't even give our FYM away.

Father sent off for as much information as he could from the various people who were advertising. It turned out that they all wanted a terrific amount of money for their worms, and father decided that, since he already had worms in his dung heaps, he could save himself some money and try worm farming in his own way. Typical farmer. A worm bed about forty feet (12m) long and three feet (90cm) wide was made out of two rows of railway sleepers. Every Sunday father went round his dung heaps with a two-gallon (9-lit.) bucket collecting worms, and, when he had half a bucket full, which took several weeks, he sprinkled these worms over the rotten manure that he had placed in the bed, covered them up with more manure and left them to it. However, when he went to check his worms several months later, father had a shock. He was hoping to find lots of compost and millions of worms, but not only was there no worm compost, there wasn't a single worm either. They had all disappeared. He then realized that he was going to have to fork out some money and buy the right sort of worms, along with a vital bit of information, and that was how to keep the little devils in the worm bed in the first place.

Father decided to take mother up to Yorkshire for a long weekend. This was unheard of. Mother thought she was going round the cathedral, antique shops and craft fairs, but father had something else in mind. On the Sunday they took a drive out into the Yorkshire Dales, the mist had come down, it was pouring with rain and eventually they arrived at this rumble-tumble-down old farm, situated in the middle of nowhere. The reason father had come here was to see a man whose company, Wonder Worms UK Ltd, sold worms as advertised in *Farmers Weekly*. These worms were supposed to be marvellous, a unique species called Californian Redworms which would do wonders for your dung heap. (There is no such thing as a Californian Redworm; it was just some marvellous name dreamed up to boost sales, and it worked an absolute treat.) Father was so taken in by this chap's enterprise that he decided to buy 20,000 worms there and then. Normally they were sold on a mail-order basis and were despatched in bathtubs covered with a perforated lid, but try as they might my father and this man could not get a bathtub in the boot of the car. They then had the brilliant idea of putting the worms in old fertilizer sacks, which they duly did. The man had kept telling my father that he must double the number of worms in his worm beds every six months, and before setting off for home father asked him how to do this. The reply came back in a thick Yorkshire brogue, 'Well lad, I gets rotavator, sticks it through worm bed, and then I gets double the number of worms'. What a callous man. Grasping this useless bit of information, my father set off for home. Needless to say, when he got back in the car, mother wasn't too happy with him. But they set off and en route decided to stop at the first service station to make sure that everything was all right in the boot. Lo and behold, it looked just like Medusa's cavern. Encouraged by the nice, dark environment and the vibrations from the road, the worms had decided to explore their new surroundings. They were hanging in ribbons from the lid of the boot; they were all over the spare tyre; they were absolutely everywhere. It looked like spaghetti gone mad. Having put them all back in their bags once, father then had to stop at every service station on the way home to repeat the operation because he was sure that otherwise the worms would have been up in the front seat with him by the time they got home.

When my father had told us he was going into worm farming, we had pulled his leg mercilessly. Did you milk them, round them up, shear them? Did they lay eggs? But when he arrived home with these little creatures he had the last laugh, for he decided that he would breed his worms on the very farm where I was milking the cows at that time. Not only that, but he decided that it would be a nice little job for me to feed and water them after work. I was horrified. A young girl like me had better things to do with my evenings than feed and water worms. But you know what fathers are like: they twist you round their little finger and you end up doing what you're told. I had to cart large wheelbarrows full of dung round to all the worm beds that had been set up, spread the material over them and then water the beds and keep them moist. I was not allowed to use a hose pipe for watering. According to the brochure father had been given on the care of worms, it made it quite clear that should a jet of water from a hosepipe land on a worm, it could seriously damage its health. I had to use a watering can instead. But when father had gone home I used to get out the hosepipe, stick my finger over the end and hope for the best. Until that is, father had an inspection day.

Father used to come up and scrabble around his worm beds, making sure the worms were producing lots of casts and were in good health. One day, he came across a worm he had never seen before and jumped to the conclusion that this was a very sick worm indeed. I was called over to have a look at it. What should have been bright red in colour, extremely healthy looking and wriggling like mad, had gone white, wouldn't move and didn't look too well. It was all my fault. Or so I was told. I really ought to take more care looking after these worms. I lost a lot of sleep over that poor worm but when I did my own research into worms a year or so later, the very first thing I did, when I got my hands on some marvellous worm books, was look up this particular type of worm (*Octolasion lacteum*) and found that it was supposed to be 'lifeless' in the first place.

Well I fed and watered them for about six months, although at the time I couldn't grasp my father's enthusiasm for the dear little creatures. In the end he took over the task himself, but when he came to selling the compost he found out what a sham this whole worm farming enterprise was. Admittedly, he had only paid £200 for the worms he bought in Yorkshire, but many other farmers were taken in by hugely expensive worm farming franchises that were on offer at that time. So desperate were they not to lose their farms, and their way of life, as a result of quotas that they grabbed at anything that would offer them a lifeline. Franchises ranged from about £5000 to £20,000, depending on how much money you wanted to put into the enterprise. The seller of the franchise guaranteed to buy back the casts produced by the worms at anything from £70 to £100 a ton. In fact what has happened is that most of the companies selling these franchises, who had jumped onto the latest bandwagon and made their money, have never been seen or heard of since. The promise of selling the compost on your behalf never materialized, and many farmers found that after a few months they were left with a few worms and not a lot else.

Anyway, to cut a long story short, my father left the worm beds to their own devices for over a year; then, when I set up my Lady Muck business in 1986, I suddenly became very interested in worms. They took on a whole new meaning, for I suddenly realized that not only could I sell my Lady Muck compost but I could also sell the worm compost that we had collected over the past few years. This of course meant that the worms represented a potential income and I decided to resurrect the worm farming industry. However, it was not that easy. Selling my Lady Muck compost was hard work enough, but when I offered the garden centres worm compost as well, they just didn't want to know. Many companies had been there before me, had sold these so-called marvellous, though extremely expensive, products to the garden centres, and in the majority of cases had ceased to trade, leaving the garden centres with goods that no one knew about, no one could promote and no one could sell. After a year or so I gave up the whole idea of worm compost, which wasn't in any case all that it was cracked up to be. It is very fine in texture (when it dries out it resembles tea leaves), it doesn't retain moisture, and the nutrient content, although higher than ordinary farmyard manure as it is enhanced by the workings of the worms' digestive tract, is not enough for the majority of plants. Another drawback is that worm casts have to be blended with other materials, such as peat and sand, in order to retain moisture and allow free drainage. On top of all that, worm farming is extremely labour intensive since you can't use any machinery, which makes for a very expensive end product. If worm farming had the potential to be really successful, perhaps one should ask why the leading horticultural companies have not made this product themselves. The answer, as I have found to my cost, is quite obvious: it is better to add lots of organic material to your garden and let the worms do the work for you because they don't charge you a penny for doing it.

In order to supplement my income in the early days, I also took to selling worms as bait for anglers. This proved to be totally unviable but it did provide a few laughs. I used to advertise in the various fishing magazines, charging around £2 for 150 worms, inclusive of first class post and packaging. Anglers are a funny bunch. I will always remember one chap who sent in an order for redworms; he didn't want any brandlings as the fish found them bitter. How the hell he knew this, goodness only knows; it really sets the imagination running riot. I used to envisage him in the river, complete with snorkel and flippers, feeding various types of worm to the fish and coming up with the conclusion that nine out of ten trout prefer redworms. Not only did anglers often want certain types of worm but they also wanted a certain length, and you can imagine that sorting them out was a time-consuming business. Aside from that, the orders would come in when you least expected them, which made the job quite a tie, especially when the worms had to be sent off straight away for a fishing match the next day. The usual mode of transport for mail-order worms was a delicatessen carton with a perforated lid. Inside I put some food and bedding for them, and in the summer an ice cube to keep them cool. They were then put in a cardboard box and sent off in the post. I was horrified to find that worms sent to Northern

Ireland and Germany – the armed forces having keen anglers amongst their ranks – used to fly to their destination, and I can only hope that they never suffered from altitude sickness.

As the Lady Muck trade grew, it took more and more of my time and I decided that, since the bait business didn't amount to much, I would concentrate on compost. However, my interest and enthusiasm for worms was not abated. Someone asked me to give a talk about Lady Muck and I decided that I would include the natural history of the earthworm in my lecture. Although I am not an expert on the subject, I felt that perhaps I could enlighten people about the work that worms do in the garden. Now I include a bit about them in most of the talks that I give around the country.

Because they are such complex little creatures, and because each species has different characteristics, there is still a lot more to be understood about worms and their effect on the environment. We all realize that they are good for our gardens, but that's about as much as we know; I wonder how many of you are aware for instance of the number of species that abound in Britain. In this chapter I can only summarize the information available and differentiate between the commoner species, but if you wish to know more about worms I suggest that you obtain the various books that are available on the subject.

There are over 1800 different species of worm in the world, each of them adapted to their own particular environment. The only places where you won't find worms are in the very cold areas, such as the Arctic and Antarctic, and the desert regions. In Britain we have twenty-eight species, which can be roughly divided into two groups. First there are the garbage eaters, the compost and dung heap worms. All worms are nomadic, moving through the environment on a hunt for food until they find a good supply. Then they will set up home and stay as long as the going remains good. The worms that people encourage in their kitchen waste and compost heaps include several species, with names such as Eisenia, Dendrobaena, Lumbricus and Allolobophora (the latter gave their name

58

to 'lob' worms, which a lot of anglers use as trout and salmon bait). I call all the worms that ingest this decomposed material 'Cedrics', just to make it easier to remember that they have a characteristic in common. Cedric the compost worm, the most colourful of the earthworms, is bright red or pink in colour, sometimes with red banding separated by lighter bands of red or creamy yellow. A brandling or tiger worm, he is a member of the Eisenia family. *Eisenia foetida* makes very nasty smells: the yellow cells between its bands contain something called coelomic fluid, and when the worm is handled, which it does not like, it defends itself by releasing this foul-smelling fluid – a bit like gone off garlic. Perhaps that is the reason why fish don't like this species. Other compost worms have orange dots in the tail area, some varieties are an irridescent purple, and there is even one worm that I have called the 'Yuppie' as it is Barbour-coat green in colour. Its proper name is *Allolobophora chlorotica*, and it is a very small worm, about an inch to an inch and a half (2.5–3.5cm) in length, generally to be found in the garden where you have placed lots of organic material. As decomposed material passes through Cedric's body, it is ground down into finer particles, its fertility value enhanced by the worm's digestive process. The casts that Cedric excretes contain all the plant nutrients and trace elements essential to plant life. No wonder Charles Darwin said that we wouldn't know the planet as we do today if it wasn't for the worm.

Compost worms are very prolific and, like other earthworms, are most active in the spring and autumn months. They are very sociable creatures and like to live a communal life, a bit like on an Israeli kibbutz. It's probably their living habits that encourage them to lay an average of two eggs a week. These eggs take approximately eleven weeks to hatch out, though if conditions are extremely favourable this sometimes decreases to five weeks. Each egg can contain anything up to five worms, although two or three is a more usual number. When the worms hatch out they are only a few millimetres in length and white in colour. As the weeks progress they acquire their species pigmentation and reach sexual maturity after forty weeks on average, when they will lay eggs themselves and start the whole cycle again. Compost worms do not have an individual burrow and lay their eggs in any moist spot available. They do not grow to the great lengths of those worms you find when digging the garden and usually only reach approximately one to four inches (2.5–10cm) in length. They live anything up to two or three years in the natural environment, but only produce eggs for just over half their total lifespan. Being so prolific, its no wonder they die young.

That extra-large anaemic worm that you find boring through the soil in the garden has a different environmental role from that of Cedric the compost worm. I call him Dirty Harry and he is a cousin of Cedric. Dirty Harry's main job in life is to aerate and drain the soil through his burrowing. He is also responsible for refining the soil, taking in large quantities of it which are then broken down into finer fragments through digestive activity. The worm casts that Dirty Harry excretes are very bland, and their nutrient content is negligible because these worms ingest only soil and the small quantity of organic matter that they need for their own personal requirements. Dirty Harry is one of the worms who

loves to leave his casts on the surface of the soil, especially on lawns and bowling greens. There are two main species responsible for this – *Allolobophora longa* and *A. nocturna* – and unfortunately nothing can be done to stop them, bar using chemicals. We ought to thank our lucky stars that their casts are very small: in Burma the giant Notoscolex worms produce skyscraper casts, some as much as eight to ten inches (20–25cm) high, and one and a half inches (4cm) in diameter, weighing in at about three pounds four ounces (1.5kg). The trouble is that, if you have a healthy soil, you won't be able to stop worms coming into it. They are effectively refining the soil for you, producing on average, according to Darwin, at least 7.5 tons of casts per acre in a layer a quarter of an inch (just over 5mm) deep every year. If you think this sounds a lot, in the Nile Valley the worms produce on average 1200 tons of casts per acre.

Dirty Harry, unlike Cedric, has his own burrow approximately eight to ten inches (20–25cm) below the surface. The burrow is thermometer-shaped, the bulbous bottom of which Dirty Harry will line with dead leaves and other organic material that he has dragged down into his home. This material gives him warmth during the winter and coolness during the summer; although worms are cold-blooded creatures, they react to warmth and cold just as we do. I expect many of you have seen leaves sticking out of the entrances of worm burrows, especially in the autumn. Dirty Harry likes to conceal his burrow from predators such as thrushes, blackbirds and robins. If they see an open worm burrow, these birds know that Dirty Harry is just below the surface and that if they peck on the soil, imitating falling rain which worms love, this will bring him out of his burrow and provide them with a tasty meal. Maybe the reason that Dirty Harrys still come to the surface in response to birds is that none of them have ever survived to go back and tell the others what exactly happens.

Being a bit of a loner, Dirty Harry mates only a few times a year. The eggs usually contain only one worm, and take anything from six months to a year to hatch out, depending on environmental conditions. The eggs are laid in the soil and remain in animated suspension until conditions are right for hatching. The baby worms are white in colour and only a few millimetres in length, and they take anything from six months to a year to mature and start to lay eggs themselves. These worms can grow to enormous lengths: I have seen them up to fifteen inches (38cm) long when they are fully extended, and I always make a note of where I have found the larger ones as I like to take them along to the talks that I give. If you whip them out very quickly at a WI meeting, you can almost guarantee that you'll have three old biddies fainting in the front row. It's great fun. You tell people that you have brought some little friends with you for the evening, and the last thing they expect you to produce is a fifteen-inch (38cm) Dirty Harry.

The largest worm in this country is the *Lumbricus terrestris*. It is also our deepest burrowing earthworm, preferring the cool, damp conditions of the subsoil and coming up to the surface only to feed. When we were doing some excavating work on our farm several years ago I found a few of these worms eight feet (2.4m) down. Mind you, we were experiencing a drought at that time, and this had probably forced the worms deeper into the soil. In very dry weather a lot of worms 'hibernate', tying themselves into a figure of eight knot in their burrows and remaining in a comatose state until more favourable environmental conditions reawaken them. If you dig your garden over in a dry summer or even winter, you will probably come across several species of Dirty Harry either tied in a knot or coiled into a ball. Don't leave them on the surface to dry out; return them to the soil or a damp spot in the garden. Dirty Harry doesn't live for a great length of time: anything up to four years is normal in the natural environment, although in captivity some species have been kept for ten years or more. The largest worm found in this country, so I have been told, was a *Lumbricus terrestris* living on the Yorkshire Moors about twenty years ago. It was twenty-eight inches (70cm) in length when fully extended. What age this worm would have been goodness knows, but certainly it would have been in double figures.

The largest species of worm is found in the state of Victoria in Australia, the *Megascolides australis* which grows up to eleven feet (3.3m) long. Its egg is about the size of a bantam's egg, or class 6. Now the Australians don't know this, but perhaps the reason why they have emus in Australia is because you'd need a damned big bird like that to pull one of these worms out of the ground. The largest worm to be found in Europe, *Hormogaster redii gigantes*, lives in the south of mainland Italy and on the island of Sicily, and it is almost as long as its name, growing up to three feet (90cm) long. I wonder if this worm had anything to do with the invention of spaghetti?

Worms were probably one of the very first creatures to make an appearance on planet earth and their fossilized remains go back millions of years, even further than the dinosaurs. But it is only in the course of the last few thousand years that we have appreciated their importance. In early Egyptian times farmers realized how important worms were for the fertility of their soil; in fact they worshipped them and treated them like gods. When the Hanging Gardens of Babylon were built, worms were introduced from the Nile delta to ensure and maintain their soil fertility. Over the years we seem to have been misinformed as to the benefits of a healthy worm

population both on farmland and in gardens. Gilbert White mentions worms and their magnificent work in his book *The Natural History and Antiquities of Selborne*, published in 1788, but it was James Samuelson in 1858 who wrote the first major work on the taxonomy of the earthworm and pointed out its environmental benefits. Interestingly enough, it seems that in the early 1800s there had been little interest in worms. In fact I have some gardening books of the time which state that any gardener worth his salt would not have a worm in the garden. They were associated with the snake in the Garden of Eden and thought to be very evil creatures indeed. Gardeners would sprinkle their lawns with slaked lime or salt, make wonderful potions based on tannin to spray on their herbaceous borders and even stamp on worms should they find one under foot. White and Samuelson did nothing to correct these harmful statements and it wasn't until Charles Darwin published his book *The Formation of Vegetable Mould through the action of Worms* in 1881 that farmers and gardeners alike developed an interest in worms and abandoned their needless slaughter of these wonderful creatures.

The earthworm does not prey upon any living thing, animal or vegetable, though it seems that everything preys upon the poor old earthworm. Eaten by carnivorous slugs, centipedes, badgers, hedgehogs, thrushes, blackbirds and robins, it also plays host to the cluster fly whose larvae parasitize it, but I suppose the main predator of the earthworm are moles. They have to eat their own body weight in earthworms every day in order to survive, and that can mean 200g or more in weight (approximately a hundred and fifty to two hundred Dirty Harrys). Moles even take precautionary steps in order to supply themselves with worms should they become ill or run out of food, or should their tunnels become waterlogged. Down in their network of tunnels, moles have a larder where they store excess Dirty Harrys. Having had their daily fill, they then go on an expedition to procure worms to put aside, biting into their necks to sever the ventral nerve, which effectively paralyzes them. The mole then takes them down to his larder, where they can stay alive for up to two weeks, providing him with access to a snack at any time of the day. When scientists have excavated these larders, they have found upwards of two hundred worms at any one time; whether they have a sell-by date on them remains to be seen.

Whilst I am on the subject of moles, I thought you might like to know that they tunnel at approximately forty-five feet (13m) an hour through light loam or sandy soils. However, during the mating season, a male mole will tunnel at 150 feet (45m) an hour to get to a female mole. It makes you wonder what sort of state he arrives in. Anyway, should you be having trouble with moles in your garden, I suggest that you throw away all those milk bottles, windmills, sonic devices and mole traps and get yourselves a nice, juicy female mole. Chuck her over the fence into your neighbours' garden and all your problems should disappear. Unfortunately, if you have a healthy worm population in your garden, then you are likely to have moles. Bar trapping and poisoning, there is no effective deterrent on offer, although I have been told that ferret dung placed in mole runs is very effective – ferrets being the mole's natural predator.

In Ireland, where they don't have moles and there was, until recently, a healthy worm population, a new type of worm, the flatworm, has made an appearance. A few years ago the Irish noticed that their worm population had become so depleted that they launched an investigation to find out the reason why. The flatworm, which they discovered was responsible for the decline in numbers, is in fact indigenous to New Zealand. It attacks earthworms by sucking out the internal organs and juices and leaving an empty shell. I read that this flatworm may have been introduced to Ireland in the early 1960s, and has therefore had time to establish itself well and truly. The Irish Ministry of Agriculture has apparently sent out a team of experts to New Zealand to discover whether or not the flatworm has a natural predator which they can then introduce to Ireland in order to control its numbers. Interestingly enough, there are one or two species of leech and a flatworm present in this country which prey upon earthworms; obviously they have their predators, otherwise their numbers would be out of control here too and we would be experiencing the dilemma facing the Irish. Dirty Harry carries several viruses, transporting them from place to place by means of burrowing. He can also act as an intermediate host for tapeworms and nematodes which then go on to infect birds and small mammals. Although it has not been proven that humans can catch, or be infected with, any viruses or nematodes as a result of contact with worms, you should always wash your hands after handling soil or working in the garden.

The worm is a very complex little creature. Even he has his off days, and I remember being told by an eminent biologist that British worms suffer from influenza as a result of our inclement climate, though I cannot find any scientific records to support this. Whilst we are on the ills affecting worms, would you believe me if I said that even worms get worms?

Although worms are hermaphrodite in that they have both male and female sexual reproductive organs, the majority of them have to mate with another worm in order to lay eggs. About halfway along their length is a band, usually slightly raised and of a different colour, known as the saddle or clitellum, which is essential to the act of reproduction. Some people believe this ring to be scar tissue formed as a result of a worm being cut in half and joined together again. When ready to copulate, the worms come together, lying head to tail, their clitellums resting against each other. The clitellum releases fluid which forms a slimy tube around each worm, and into this the fertilized cell is ejected. Copulation takes approximately one hour. The worms then break away, each with a fertilized cell on the clitellum, and move backwards while the slimy tube moves forwards over the worm's head to form a cocoon. When freshly laid, these cocoons look like green lemons and, as the gestation period progresses, the egg changes colour, eventually becoming a reddish-brown by the time the worms are ready to hatch out. Unlike birds and reptiles, they have a birth canal along which they venture into the outside world. You would have to look very closely at your compost heaps and soil to see these eggs, which are only a couple of millimetres long and resemble a seed pod. Worm eggs are not to be confused with the large, round, white eggs of snails and slugs; these require the thumbscrew treatment.

Since I don't wish to bore you to death with an in-depth analysis of the worm's taxonomy, I'll keep the biology lesson brief. The worm effectively eats his way through the soil, taking matter into his mouth by sucking it in – he has no teeth – a bit like a hoover. The food passes through the pharynx into the oesophagus, on through the gizzard where it is ground down, and then into the alimentary canal, a long continuous tube, at the end of which a cast is excreted. From the worm's brain extends the nerve cord, the equivalent of our spinal cord. The worm, which has no ears and no eyes, is dependent on vibration, and relies on the many nerve endings in the body wall to react to different stimuli and pass sensory messages to the brain. One stimulus to which worms seem to respond is that of falling rain. This falls in a rhythmic pattern and brings them to the surface as it provides them with ideal conditions in which to move around. After excessive rain thousands of worms have often been found lying dead on top of the soil. Drowning has been ruled out as worms can survive in water for several days, but perhaps the build up in the soil of gases such as hydrogen sulphide is responsible, or perhaps these worms were sick in the first place and were washed out of their homes, too weak to plug their burrows. Though blind, worms do react to light by means of light-sensitive receptors in their heads. Ultra violet rays are extremely harmful to worms, hence their need to work in the dark, deep down in the soil. Should they be exposed to daylight as a result of your digging the garden, worms retreat to the depths very quickly; they do not like being disturbed at all. The Lumbricus earthworm has five hearts, not the hearts that you and I have but cardiovascular rings which pump the blood around the body. They also have organs called nephridia, which are very similar to kidneys, a bladder and chloragogen cells which act like a mobile liver. Worms do not have lungs; they breathe through their skin, which is kept moist at all times by various glands. Oxygen permeates through the skin to the blood vessels, where it is taken up by the haemoglobin in the blood and passed around the body, hence the worm's ability to live in water for several days. There are two pairs of setae, or bristles, on each segment except the very first one in the head area. These setae help the worm move through the soil, and, more importantly, they help him to remain in his burrow when being pulled out of the ground by a bird. The setae dig into the wall of the burrow and hold fast, and the worm will literally be pulled in two before letting go.

Finally, the old wives' tale about cutting a worm in half and getting two has not yet been proved. If you sever a worm in two in the head area, then more often than not it will be killed outright as the major organs of the body will have been damaged. I have found that if you cut the worm in half in the tail area, the segment tends to heal and the worm carries on living, though I haven't found any proof that the tail end suddenly develops five hearts, a bladder and all the other organs at the drop of a hat in order to survive. The pronounced wriggling of the tail is due to the specialized nerve endings which react violently, sometimes for many days, after being severed. At least forty per cent of worms seem to die from shock as a result of being cut in two, which is hardly surprising. If someone came along and cut you in half with a dirty great spade, you might suffer from shock as well. But don't become paranoid about digging the garden. As I have mentioned, worms do not like to be disturbed and, as soon as you thrust that spade or fork into the ground, they will be off as fast as their little segments can carry them. Please do not do as one lady did a few years ago when she unintentionally cut a worm in half: she was so upset that she tried to save it by joining it back together again with a sticking plaster. The poor worm hadn't a hope of surviving this operation and, to make matters worse, it was shoved into a dry old matchbox. When the victim was handed over to me, all the box contained were two bits of very small stick, one of which had a dirty great plaster flapping on it. Every dead worm provides approximately ten milligrams of nitrogen to the soil and, when you think that you may have a couple of hundred worms per cubic metre in the soil, one little worm is not to be missed. Worms thrive on pastureland, the grass providing food and a sanctuary from the elements and from predators. Artificial fertilizers do not affect worm populations, as many people believe; in fact an increased nitrogen content in the soil results in some cases in increased numbers. Worms will be harmed by pesticides and herbicides in concentrated form, but only if they feed on infected material, which will of course produce a knock-on effect on the wildlife population that feeds on these worms. Thankfully, the use of pesticides and herbicides is declining rapidly in this country, although, amazingly, gardeners spend twice as much on chemicals as do farmers.

CEDRIC'S RECIPE FOR SUCCESSFUL COMPOST

At my talks I am often asked how I managed to make a compost utilizing worms. It seems that many people have tried the various techniques on offer but all have failed. First of all, making worm compost is not that easy; you are dealing with creatures that react to their environment in different ways, and worms can be quite fussy about what they eat: the simpler the food available the faster they'll ingest it. What you have to remember is that it will take some time to achieve the dark, rich, humic material that they eventually produce. Depending on the material in use, it can take a year or longer to make a worthwhile amount of compost. Because a compost bin used for worms is much smaller than an ordinary compost heap (less than three feet – 90cm – square), there is no danger of heat building up. The bin should be placed directly on the ground to allow movement between soil and compost and free drainage. Into this bin can be placed most of your kitchen waste, including of course vegetable and fruit waste. If you want to have a successful worm bin, then look at it from the worm's point of view. What does he eat in his natural environment? The answer is decomposed material, such as leaves and vegetable matter. You won't find him in a pile of newspapers, in a bag of peat or asleep in a straw bale. You will find him underneath cow pats or anywhere decomposed material has been allowed to gather. The more natural the material and the more advanced its state of decomposition, the more readily ingested it is and the more appealing to the worm. Don't throw him a fresh cabbage leaf and tell him to get on with it. Firstly, worms don't have any teeth; all matter has to be broken down by bacteria before they can suck it in. Even when we fed them on pure cow muck – vegetable waste broken down by bacterial activity in the cow – it took up to a week for the worms to approach this material and ingest it. Once there, however, we had a job to stop them, and wonderful compost they made of it too. One way of speeding up worm bin activity is to feed worms shredded material. Either put your waste through a shredder, break it into small pieces by hand, or do as a friend of mine did and put your kitchen waste in the liquidizer. This produced quite spectacular results.

HOW TO MAKE A VERY SIMPLE WORM BED

Over the years I have used various materials for making worm beds. The most effective were made of wood, which provides warmth. When we first started worm farming we used railway sleepers, which offered both warmth and shelter, but sleepers are difficult to come by today and, since they are eight feet (2.4m) long, do take up a lot of room. Two rows of sleepers were placed three feet (90cm) apart and into the bottom of the space between we placed some lovely rotten manure. Too much straw is bad news for worms as the straw takes all the nitrogen out of the surrounding area to break itself down before releasing it. Worms also require a lot of nitrogen in order to grow and reproduce, so make sure you do not put shrubby material in your worm bed. Worms were then sprinkled over the bed and covered with two to three inches (5–8cm) of manure. Sacking was put over the top as it is most important to keep the manure moist, though not soaking wet, and to encourage the worms to move around in the manure and ingest it without being affected by harmful ultra-violet light. Following this method will allow them to break down the manure far more quickly. Every week an inspection should be made. If the material is too dry, moisten it well. If the worms are into that top layer of manure then add another couple of inches but, before doing so, turn over the top layer using a fork. This ensures that any undigested material is turned under so that it can become more acceptable to the worms; it also aerates the bed and encourages worm activity. As the weeks progress you will notice that, however much muck you put on the worm bed, it never seems to overflow. Instead it tends to sink. This is a sure sign that the worms are enjoying the material, and if you delve down to the bottom of the bed you should find an almost black, gritty material – the wormcasts.

After about a year you should have a fair amount of material to harvest from your worm bed. Now for the hard bit. How do you get the compost out without the worms? What I used to do was feed the worms some bran, just lightly sprinkled over the worm bed as too much can cause digestive problems. The bran would draw ninety per cent of the worms into the top eight inches (20cm) of the worm bed, which contained fresh and semi-digested material. I allowed two to three days for this to happen, and then shovelled off the top eight inches (20cm) of compost. This dark material was placed on the floor of a shed and spread to a depth of six inches (15cm) or more, which enabled the compost to dry out quickly. As it dried, the top layer was skimmed off and placed in sacks until required. The two-inch (5cm) bottom layer, which was left on the floor, was quite wet and contained all the worms that we hadn't managed to leave behind in the bed. This material would be used for the basis of a new bed, having had some fresh manure added on top to provide food for the worms, but it can be returned to the original bed when the operation is completed. The worm compost itself was used mainly for potting as we found that, if we put large quantities of it around the garden, not only did it sprout one or two weeds because it had not been sterilized but it also deterred worms from that area. The reason for this was that, like any other animal, a worm will not ingest its own manure, and since the compost failed to provide the worm with any food it was unattractive to them.

The above section describes how to make compost using manure but you can apply exactly the same method to waste vegetable matter; please remember though that it is a long process. The best environment for the worm is out in the open, where he can come and go as he pleases. If the worm does not like certain substances, he will tell you by not ingesting them. These substances include poultry manure, straw, spicy and shiny leaves such as laurel, camellia and rhododendron, and hard, dry materials such as pine needles, bark and wood shavings. Citrus fruit skins don't go down too well either.

Many people these days are selling worm bins. These are just glorified dustbins, with a drainage tap inserted at the bottom (to release the moisture which is a partial effect of the waste breaking down) and a tiny hole in the lid. This hole is covered with mesh to stop flies getting in and perhaps the worms getting out, thereby forcing them to adapt to their environment, like it or not. The trouble with these bins is that they are not natural; they don't allow the material to breathe or enough moisture to escape. This of course encourages an anaerobic state in which worms will not breed; nor will they ingest the waste too readily. Remember, the material you feed to them has to be several months old before they will accept it, so don't put worms in one of these dustbins without a plentiful supply of decomposed material. If adding worms to a compost heap outside, it is worthwhile first putting them in half a bucket of the material on which you intend them to feed. Cover it with a perforated lid to stop them getting out and place it in a light spot, though never in sunlight, for several days. The light will keep them in the bucket. This will give the worms a chance to adapt to their new environment before you place them in your compost heap or worm bed. Otherwise the chances are they will not like their new surroundings and will clear off. Many worms sold in angling shops have been reared on muck, and having to adapt to a vegetable compost heap is a bit of a shock.

So the most effective way of speeding up the worm composting process is to give them material that is easily ingested and to keep the heap covered with old carpet or sacking. I don't like polythene as it tends to keep the moisture in and prevent the heap from breathing properly; it can also look very untidy. Keeping the worms in the dark will encourage them to work; its their natural environment. Never add lime or any compost activator to your heap or bin if you want to encourage worms as these materials can prove to be a little abrasive for the poor little fellows. You shouldn't have to buy any worms for your bin or heap if you are making compost of any quality as the worms will be in there before you know it; they know a good thing when they see it. You can collect worms by looking under bits of wood or stone or around the edges of dung heaps and compost heaps, even under piles of leaves. Anywhere decomposed material has gathered you will find Cedric and his friends partying away.

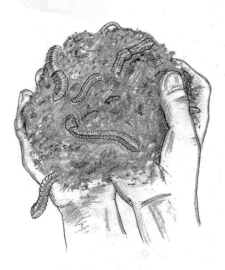

CHAPTER FIVE

MUCK THROUGH
THE AGES

*The tree of liberty must be refreshed from time to time
with the blood of patriots and tyrants.
It is its natural manure.*

PRESIDENT THOMAS JEFFERSON (1743–1826)

We all take for granted the many
different kinds of artificial fertilizers, manures, composts and soil
conditioners on offer today. But how many of you have ever wondered what they used in the past in order to grow crops and
vegetables? In this chapter I hope to bring to your attention the
various materials that have been used for this purpose through the
ages and what brought about their introduction as fertilizers.

Where, first of all, did the idea of manuring the land come
from? And how did people find out that manure was essential for
plant growth? As mentioned in Chapter Three, the Mesopotamians
used to flood the plains of the rivers Tigris and Euphrates in order
to fertilize their soil. The longer the flood water remained over the
land, the better the soil became as a result of the vast quantities of
rich silt it absorbed. In Greek mythology manure, of all things,
crops up in various legends and, as these are based on life at that
time, they are one way of learning about the past. For example,
one of the Twelve Labours of Hercules was to clean out the stables
of Augeas, King of Elis, in which three thousand oxen were housed.
It had not been cleaned for over thirty years – I'd hate to think
what it looked like – and the task had to be completed in a single
day. Hercules's solution was to divert the rivers Alpheus and Peneus
through the cow stalls, thereby washing away the manure built up
over three decades. It is to this procedure of washing out the
manure with water that the instigation of both irrigation and
fertilization are attributed. The date of the legend is not known,
but Homer's *Odyssey*, written in about 700 BC, mentions that
Laertes, the father of Odysseus, spread manure from his dung
heaps on his vineyards. The Greeks seemed to have had a good
understanding of nature and the importance of a healthy soil.
Between 435 and 354 BC the Athenian military leader and historian

Xenophon observed that his estate had been impoverished as a result of the workers' ignorance in not manuring the land, which prompted him to say that there is nothing quite so good as manure. Theophrastus, a Greek philosopher who followed in Xenophon's footsteps, recommended the abundant use of manure on poor soils but that rich soils should be manured sparingly. He also advocated using bedding for stables and cow stalls, a practice still in use today, and said that the bedding would conserve the goodness of the muck and increase the humic value of the manure. Sewage from the city of Athens was used in gardens and olive groves and was sold to farmers, having been transported to the country by means of a network of canals. Liquid manures, made by dissolving manure in water, were spread on the vineyards and olive groves as well. The Greeks classified manures according to their richness: Theophrastus listed human ordure at the top, with swine, goat, sheep, cow, oxen and horse manure following in that order. Varro, a Roman agriculturalist, adjusted this list a few years later, replacing human manure at the top with poultry manure, which he found far superior. And to enrich the manure in the first place, Columella, a Roman notary, recommended feeding cattle on clover.

But it wasn't only manure they used on the land. Ancient civilizations also recognized the benefits to be derived from the decomposed flesh of dead animals and humans and, more importantly, from their blood. This has already been mentioned in Chapter Three in connection with the twelfth-century Moor Ibn-al-Awam, who believed that there was nothing to compare with the effectiveness of human blood as a fertilizer. *The Rubaiyat of Omar Khayyám* makes the same point:

> *I sometimes think that never blows so red*
> *The Rose as where some buried Caesar bled;*
> *That every Hyacinth the Garden wears*
> *Dropt in her Lap from some once lovely Head.*

In more recent times the use of human and animal remains as a manure is mentioned in Richard Bradley's *General Treatise of Husbandry and Gardening* of 1726. The author was particularly fond of using 'animal flesh', placing it directly under the roots when planting. The results were excellent. Bradley also found soap quite successful as a manure. The diplomat and essayist Sir William Temple decreed that his heart be buried in his garden when he died, and Thomas Hollis, of Corscombe in Dorset, ordered that his body be buried in one of his fields and that the field was immediately to be ploughed. This act of love for one's own little bit of England has been immortalized in the Revd William Crowe's poem entitled 'Lewesdon Hill':

> *Fain would I view thee, Corscombe, fain would view*
> *The ground where Hollis lies; his choice retreat,*
> *Where, from the busy world withdrawn, he lived*
> *To generous Virtue and the holy love*
> *Of liberty a consecrated Spirit;*
> *And left his ashes there; still honouring*
> *Thy fields with title given of patriot names,*
> *But more with his untitled sepulchre*
> *That envious ridge conceals thee from my sight*
> *Which passing o'er thy place north east, looks on*
> *To Sherborne's ancient towers.*

Of course many people have had their hearts buried in the land that they loved most, and human remains have enriched the soil since ancient times. The Chinese have been using bones as a manure for thousands of years, and after the Napoleonic Wars we imported from Holland quantities of bonemeal made from the remains of both horses and men killed in battle at Waterloo and Leipzig. In 1833 Archibald Gorrie, a gardener from Annat in Scotland, used this bonemeal only once before he found out what it contained, after which he never did so again, but many people brushed aside the notion that it was offensive to use bonemeal made from dead men's bones, remarking that the soldiers would have been only too glad that their remains were being put to use; after all, it was one way of coming home to England and living on in the fertility of the soil. (I think if this happened today the reaction would be similar to that of Archibald Gorrie, namely one of horror and outrage.) This bonemeal, which proved very effective on turnip crops in Scotland, was first introduced in the East Lothian area in the 1790s by a Mr Sherrief of Captain Head, who had rollers attached to his threshing machine for grinding the bones. Mr Watson of Kieller Farm, near Cupar, said that the bones had been a great blessing to the breeders and feeders of cattle in his district and had saved the industrious tenant from ruin. Lincolnshire was one of the main English counties using bonemeal, which was brought into Louth from Holland, and in the late 1790s at Brotherless, near Boston, a steam engine was employed by a Major Cartwright for crushing bones. The Dutch extracted the glutinous

74

substance from these bones and converted it into carpenters' glue and soup cakes. Although the English recognized bones as a better manure than lime, they considered the Dutch too blinkered in their outlook, and spent much time in assiduously collecting other kinds of manure. Perhaps they had a conscience. However, a few years later the Royal Society of Sciences in Copenhagen offered a prize of a hundred crowns for the best essay on the use of bones as a manure. And in the 1840s farmers on the continent became so alive to the advantages of bonemeal and bones that a duty was laid upon their exportation; after that our imports declined.

Bonemeal is still in use today and proves to be a very valuable source of nitrogen. In their natural state bones are slow-acting and for this reason are normally crushed into bonemeal or bone flour. What you tend to buy in the garden centres is bonemeal made as a by-product of the soap-making industry or the slaughterhouse. The bones are steamed or boiled in order to remove the fat for soap, and the residue is then crushed to make bonemeal. This is commonly used in today's composts, where it provides not only nitrogen but also a very high proportion of phosphate. Broken bones are also processed to make glue and the residue is ground finely to produce bone flour. There used to be a product on the market called greaves, which consisted of meat, cartilage and bonemeal combined. It was sold as a cheap substitute for dried blood and originated as a by-product from tallow (used in the making of soap and candles). Apparently the smell was unbelievably awful. Dried blood was thought to be especially valuable, and this belief was confirmed when the poor soil on which a battle between the Cavaliers and Roundheads took place yielded bountiful crops for many years. Today dried blood is used for its high nitrogen content and fast-acting potency.

The use of hoof and horn goes back many centuries. The rector John Worlidge (1630–93) wrote that if you put the hooves, horns and skins of dead cattle in a pit with some shreds of tanned leather, hair, salt of the oak bark and lime from the bones of the beast, mixed it with an equal proportion of earth and watered it occasionally, it would make an excellent compost for your kitchen garden. He also recommended hoof parings, soaked in water for approximately a month, as a liquid manure. He was very much a soil enthusiast and wanted to create soils in this country that compared with the rich, fertile soils to be found in the Nile Valley. He was convinced that one of the very first steps towards achieving this was to screen your soil, getting rid of weeds, stones and, above all, worms 'that do so annoy'. Like other farmers, he was very keen on the use of woollen rags as a fertilizer. These were obtained from recently deceased paupers in London (farmers would pay ten times as much for a load of rags as for a load of dung), and old people and widows were employed to cut the rags into small pieces. No farmer would handle them himself for fear of catching the pox. The rags would then be ploughed in and, as they disintegrated, would feed the soil – at least, that was the theory.

The use of animal manure on the land goes back many centuries, but the earliest writings I can find that suggest which time of year one should spread this pabulum, or food, of the soil are in *The English Husbandman* of 1613, written by Gervase Markham. He suggested manuring the land from April to May, the best materials being cow, horse and sheep dung, all excellent for breaking up clay soil. If these were unavailable, then black mud from the bottom of ponds or the straw spread on wet highways, if shovelled up when well trampled and put into heaps to ferment a while, would both serve as alternatives, the spring being the ideal time to do this. Dung from all types of fowl was acceptable, but pigeon dung, crumbled and sown with the wheat, was the best for immediate results. According to Markham, floor sweepings could also be used in the fields and garden, but one should take great care not to have any 'stinking or muddy dikes' or dung hills in the garden or near the house, 'whose smells and evil vapours not only corrupt and breed infection in man but also cankers which kill and consume all manner of plants'. More manure should be added and dug in in

September and November, using only the finest cow and horse manure available, preferably material aged for two years. Like so many others, our friend Gervase Markham did not like worms, and caterpillars he considered to be 'filthy little worms'. His recipe for getting rid of earthworms was to burn horse manure to ashes, mix it with earth, and use this as a medium in which to plant seeds. It would kill the worms and encourage the plants.

Different manures did different things for your plants, and gardeners preferred the dung from fattening hogs or swine for their soft fruit. Horse dung was the principle ingredient for hotbeds, in which were grown pineapples, other exotic fruits and vegetables, citrus trees and mushrooms. Horse manure was 'hot' because horses were probably the only animals which were fed on corn and which therefore produced rich excrement; as their digestive tract is not very long, only partial fermentation takes place before food matter is excreted. Cow dung, which comes out fully broken down but not as rich as horse dung because a diet of forage is relatively poor, was considered to be 'cold' and was mainly used in the vegetable garden. It was recommended that, when delivered fresh, it should be placed in a moist, warm spot, and turned often to make a really good compost. Today cow manure is probably the finest material one can use. The Dutch are very keen on it and look at their horticultural industry today.

Human waste was the principle manure used by the Chinese for thousands of years and, indeed, still is today. In fact for a long time

a law of the State made it illegal to throw away this valuable material, and people were employed to collect it from houses and take it to the paddy fields and gardens, where it was put to good use. To this day human ordure, or night soil, is still the principle manure used to fertilize the crops that feed China's millions. Very few domestic animals are kept, with the exception of the odd oxen to pull ploughs, pigs which eat left-overs, and chickens, ducks and pigeons which are kept for the table. Until the last century the practice of recycling human waste was also commonplace on the Continent, but in this country we had some absurd idea that it gave plants an unpleasant flavour. Well, it couldn't be worse than eating cabbages grown in goat manure, according to Mr Alex Forsyth in 1870, who said that when boiled they had the rank smell of a billy goat.

It was gradually realized that all the human waste flowing into the Thames was a great loss to farmer and gardener alike, and it was proposed in the 1820s that aqueducts should be built to transport the sewage to the countryside (someone else had been reading their Greek mythology). It was then decided that these aqueducts could induce malaria, and in the 1820s a huge plan was devised for a treatment works near Battersea, in London. This was superseded by a better plan to construct a building at the mouth of each sewer, fifty to sixty feet (15m by 18m) high and fifty to a hundred feet (15m by 30m) wide. Inside would be thirty to forty layers of mesh laid a foot (30cm) apart, each layer progressively finer, the mesh at the top having apertures one inch (2.5cm) across while that at the bottom would be a fraction of this. On the floor of the building would be a huge sponge. Sewage would be pumped to the top by means of a steam engine, and would percolate down through the layers of mesh. An interval of an hour would be allowed in the course of the operation in which to scrape off the solid matter from each layer. This would then be put into boxes, compressed and placed to dry in a separate building, where the manure or poudrette cakes, as they were known, could be used for fuel, to make walls or as fertilizer in the countryside. Any bones present in the solid matter would be scraped off the mesh as well and put through a bone crusher or mill. It was thought that this method would eventually produce water wholesome enough to be used for domestic purposes, which at that time, it wasn't. Mind you, things haven't changed much. Every time I ask for a glass of water at a friend's house in London, I am told the number of pairs of kidneys that the water has been through before it goes through mine. It doesn't put me off; at least we are able to have water from a tap, and many in the world are not so lucky. As for the taste, well, if you look at the size of London and work out how many miles of pipe this water has to travel, it's no wonder that it has its own peculiar flavour.

In the past market gardeners around London used vast amounts of human ordure from the sewers, and in more recent times the Leatherhead sewage works has earned a reputation for sewage beyond compare. Everywhere I go to give one of my talks I meet people who have acquired dried sewage sludge for their gardens from the Leatherhead works. Several years ago, with the introduction of peat-free products, sewage sludge made a short comeback in popularity. This coincided with the ban on straw and stubble burning, a practice regarded for centuries as an effective way of simultaneously producing potash for the soil and sterilizing it by destroying weeds and diseases. In response to the new regulations, excess straw was sprayed with sewage sludge and the final product sold as a peat alternative. Don't expect the many products using sewage to look like peat. Pure, dried sewage sludge and straw looks very much like a heavy, fine loam: there is no smell to it and, if you have a shortage of soil in your garden, this is the ideal material to bulk it up. Only sewage from rural areas which has not been contaminated by industrial waste or heavy metals can be used, however, so that the soil ecology and the plant life are protected. Around us in Somerset sewage sludge is injected into the fields with no side effects – we've even used it ourselves – but lime often has to be spread on the land to neutralize its effects. The sludge is such a powerful manure that it has the tendency to lock up certain elements in the soil, and the lime prevents this happening.

Many people are worried about the risk of disease from using sewage, but the tractor drivers and handlers who operate the machinery are a very healthy bunch, and I haven't heard of anyone catching anything nasty from handling sewage, let alone dropping down dead. We just seem to have the idea that using our own waste is not very nice, and even I have to admit that I would rather handle cow manure, but I suppose its what you have been brought up with. If we utilized all the waste matter we produced and stopped using chemicals (except in cases of dire necessity) I wonder how healthy the nation would be. Would our immune system be stronger? Certainly the Chinese are a very healthy lot, in spite of the fact that the practice over there is to pay the doctor to keep you well; only when you fall ill do you stop paying, the doctor having failed in his duty. And there are many other peoples throughout the world who recycle their own waste and do not suffer from the various commonplace ailments that plague our society. The trouble is that we live in a sterile society today in which everything has to be squeaky clean. In some respects this is not a bad thing, but I was always told that a little bit of dirt won't do you any harm.

Prior to the discovery of naturally occurring deposits of potassium in 1839, wood ash had been used as a fertilizer throughout Europe for hundreds of years, and was held to be a very important manure during the seventeenth, eighteenth and nineteenth centuries. Potash derives its name from the white residue obtained when ashes from the fire were dissolved in a pot of water. The potassium carbonate that formed was then left to dry and was sprinkled over the land much like lime. If you wanted a rich potash then you burnt beech trees, but, if they were not available, oak trees were regarded as better than nothing, although their leaves contained far more potash than the burnt wood, especially in the spring months. Wood ash was also imported from Canada, whose vast forests were more than able to meet the demands of the United Kingdom. In the 1840s the Germans used nothing but wood ash on their grasslands, and the saying was that, wherever potash was made, it should receive as much care as one gave to money, for it was a very valuable substance.

Coal ash was also used as manure for several hundred years in this country, mainly on clover and sandy grasslands, where it was quite effective, but up in bonny Scotland it seemed to do more harm than good. When used purely as a potting compost, coal ash was found to be detrimental to the root systems of house plants (this isn't surprising) and, although several trials were made, it was clear that the best use of coal ash to the gardener was as a bed on which to place potted plants: it stopped any encroaching weeds and also stopped injurious worms from entering the pots. Of course today we use coal ash or cinders as one way of stopping those nasty little creatures called slugs from engulfing our gardens; the dryness and coarseness of the ash keeps them at bay.

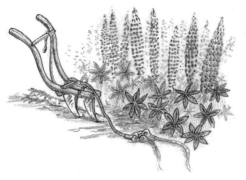

'Green' manures are used as part of a fallow ley, where the ground is not left bare but is planted with a crop that gives vital nutrients to the soil when ploughed in. These manures were used by the Romans on poor soils. Columella suggests sowing lupin seeds by 16 September, then leaving them until they have reached the required height and ploughing them in before they flower; this was thought to be one of the finest manures of all. White mustard was also used by the Romans, and is very much advocated by organic gardeners today. Other green manures used in the past include borage, the use of which was first seen in Bavaria in the 1790s. It was sown in April and ploughed in in August, and was always followed by wheat in order to obtain maximum benefits from the manure. Tatarian buckwheat (*Polygonum tataricyl*), strongly recommended by farmers and gardeners of yesteryear, was also used mainly in Germany where again it was ploughed in as a manure. Over the years all manner of plants have been used to make manure, including nettles, thistles, ragwort and potato stems. One of the most unusual green manures I have come across was made from box (*Buxus sempervirens*). This was used in France and recommended to gardeners in this country by a M. Olivier de Serres who advocated its use for the cultivation of grapes. The branches and leaves of the shrub were mulched around the vines, and their decomposition produced much valuable mould. So that's where all our parterres went.

Perhaps the origin of the word 'muck' is 'murc', the name given to the remains of the cider pressings and rotten fruit which were left in a heap to compost for nearly a year in order that any seeds should die. Today, apple pulp is fed to dairy cows and is quite sought after. In our local village we have a traditional cider factory dating back to the sixteenth century, and, at cider-making time in the autumn, the old farmer up the road is up and down like a yo-yo collecting the pulp mats. The pulp itself smells wonderful and the cows thrive on it.

In Ireland furze tops were used in the past for bedding down cattle, and, when trampled in with muck and straw, they made a marvellous manure and boosted potato crops no end. A shame that this could not have saved the Irish from their famine in the 1840s.

Tobacco was grown in this country by gardener and cottager alike. Mixed with garden mould, it was renowned for enriching the soil and was thought to contain a volatile nitrous salt used in the tanning of leather. Tobacco was regarded as a considerable asset on many country farms and of great benefit to the nation in general, of far more use as a fertilizer, it was thought, than serving its more usual purpose. Was there the first inkling of an anti-smoking campaign in the early 1800s? Tobacco water, made by soaking tobacco in water, was a very effective pesticide in Georgian green-houses. In France, where a lot of tobacco was grown, rape seed oil, mixed with horse and cow dung or vegetable waste, was used to fertilize the crop, and rape cake is utilized in a similar fashion today. (If rape seed is contaminated by mustard seed, it is considered to be unfit for cattle consumption and is then made into cakes and used as manure.) Interestingly enough, Russian comfrey, which is such a popular manure among organic gardeners today, was orig-inally used as animal fodder when in 1830 it made its first appear-ance in gardening journals. I can't find any records to support the fact that it was used before that as a manure. Other Russian delicacies included something called Potash of Russia. This was made by burning the roots of Scots fir. The ashes were then put in casks and exported all over Europe.

Another waste material used as a fertilizer was soot. Columella suggests that during Roman times turnip seed was mixed with soot and sprinkled with water the day before sowing. The soot was not only supposed to be a good manure but also an effective deterrent to turnip fleas; it was therefore advisable to sow the turnip seed whilst naked in order to stop the fleas harbouring in your clothes and being passed on to other crops. With the amount of turnip seed sown in this country I'm glad that this is not a requirement today. I already have enough problems trying to avoid looking over other people's hedges while I'm driving; the distraction of seeing some strapping farmer out sowing turnips in his birthday suit could be fatal. Sir Humphry Davy, of miner's lamp fame, was a very keen gardener, farmer and scientist, and he too found soot to be effective as a manure because of the large quantity of ammonia it contains. Newcastle coal was thought to produce the finest soot, but in London the sweeps adulterated the soot by mixing it with road sweepings etc, a practice to be avoided at all cost. Soot was mainly used as a top dressing but a Mr Robertson of Kilkenny, Ireland, gardener to the gentry, found it to be an excellent liquid manure when mixed with water.

As an island race, one of our main industries years ago was fishing, and people living around the famous fish market of Billingsgate used fish guano to manure their gardens and nurseries. Very rich in nitrogen and phosphates, fishmeal is available today in garden centres; although it does have rather a sweet, fishy smell, any discomfort to the olfactory senses is far surpassed by the unpleasantness of actually handling it. Sprats were thought to make the ideal guano, and in early Victorian times they were pressed to extract the oil. The remains, consisting of bones, scales etc, were known as sprat oilcake. This was used extensively around the Medway region, where it was spread on hop grounds at a rate of thirty to fifty bushels an acre for a total cost of six or seven pence. Sprats, herrings, pilchards and other fish remains were also exported to the Continent for use as manure. Many gardeners blended sprat oilcake with earth, peat or wood ash and made a very effective compost. Whale guano, also quite common in the last century, was sold – mainly to farmers – by the cart load, one whale carcass yielding a ton of fertilizer. But if you thought a ton of fertilizer from a whale was a lot, what about the farmer who, in 1830, covered his dead carthorse with peat and, having left it for a couple of years to compost, reckoned that the horse had yielded him twenty tons of manure?

Other guanos used in this country were bird guanos from Peru and Africa, which consisted mainly of seabird dung and remains, including feathers, and were found in vast quantities under sea cliffs. Darwin makes mention of this in his writings during his travels in *The Beagle*. Guano from Peru was very dry and high in nitrogen while that from Africa was wet and high in phosphate, so two grades were available to the connoisseur. The first load of this material imported to Britain came from Peru in 1840. Bat guano was brought in from Austria, Siam, Morocco and Mexico, but it was of very poor quality and difficult to extract from the caves where it was to be found. Very little guano is imported by this country today, I suppose because our own production of various poultry manures for the garden market has superseded it.

Untried earth, bog earth, mould earth, Bruyères earth in France, turbary in Wales, turf in Ireland: these are just a sample of some of the lovely names used for peat over the centuries. Mixed with all sorts of materials from manure to fish guano, from human ordure to rape seed oil, peat was first mentioned in Stuart times for its usefulness in the garden. It has also been used for centuries as a fuel by cottagers. So all this fuss that peat has only been used since the Second World War is a load of nonsense. I still use it because there is nothing like it. Inert, acidic, moisture-retentive, fibrous, disease-free, it is the ideal substrate to produce the ideal compost. When you consider that in Ireland ninety per cent of the peat dug is burnt in power stations, effectively going up in smoke, how many people have you heard campaigning against this? The fact is that Ireland does not have any other natural resources and, surrounded by bogs, the people are only utilizing what they have as we have utilized our coal and oil. But coal and oil are not so visible and out of sight is out of mind. We have no right, however, to impose our attitudes on another country. I always remember reading in a national newspaper at the time of the pit closures that some bright chap had come up with the idea that we exchange with the Irish a shipload of coal for a shipload of peat.

We only import five per cent of the peat dug in Ireland, and this goes into horticultural use. If it wasn't for that peat, then our nurseries and garden centres would be poorer places. I totally accept that spreading peat willy-nilly round the garden is an absolute waste as there are many other materials produced in Britain that can be used in place of it, but the rumour that there is a shortage of peat is unfounded, especially if one takes a world view of the matter. There may be a shortage of English sedge peat for compost production, but there is definitely not a shortage in the world at large. Britain and Ireland together have only a very small area of bog, somewhere around four per cent of our total land mass. Sixty-four per cent of the world's peat bogs are to be found in Russia, and you can in fact buy Russian peat in this country, although it is very fibrous since the Russians don't have the machinery to refine it. Scandinavian countries are also very rich in peat bogs. The beauty of sphagnum moss peat is that it does grow back again, albeit at only two millimetres a year, but it is growing so rapidly in Finland that they are drowning in the stuff and can't even give it away. Canada and Alaska also have millions of acres of peat bog, and many compost companies in this country have purchased land there in order to supply their own demand. So you see, we would have to use sphagnum moss peat at a phenomenal rate before it ran out. Clearly it should be used for the purpose for which it has gained its reputation, and that is as an excellent medium in which to grow the vast array of plants that help to maintain our beautiful green environment and give us all so much pleasure.

Having given you my side of the peat debate, I will now tell you about the history of coir or coconut fibre, which is being imported into this country in order to help preserve peat bogs. Coconut trees were known to the Georgians and were even grown in large conservatories in the early 1800s, but coconut fibre was first brought to the public's attention as a good mulching material in 1862, in the September edition of *The Gardener's Chronicle and Agricultural Gazette*. Coconut fibre had been in use in the 1850s in the coir matting, brush-making and rope industries (the nuts, having been brought into this country in their whole state, underwent various processes to extract whatever was necessary to the manufacture of the end product). Fibre for mulching, however, was made available in 1862 by the Cocoa-nut Fibre Company at Kingston upon Thames, and sold for the princely sum of three shillings a horse load. The London Manure Company, established in 1840, was selling coconut dust as a mulch for forty shillings a ton by 1870, though its use declined over the years. As British men went to fight in the various wars that raged in the Commonwealth, fewer gardeners were available to produce the exotic fruits and vegetables that had found their way to many a country house table in the course of the 1800s. People also left the land in vast numbers, finding work in industrial towns and cities, and it gradually became cheaper to import certain food products into this country than to grow them ourselves. With the introduction of refrigeration on ships, cheap food imports have flooded the market. The appearance of coir in Britain in the last few years has made me wonder why we import all this stuff from thousands of miles away when surely the countries of origin – India, Sri Lanka, Africa, etc, which are considered to be Third World countries, have more need of it than we do. It's amazing that it is not used in those countries to feed the people who need it most. Just think of all the fossil fuel used in bringing it here in the first place. At least moss peat only has to come fifty-six miles across the Irish Sea from Ireland and not a great deal further from Scandinavia. Of the many peat alternatives available in this country, it is worth mentioning a wonderful product called cocoa shell; a by-product of the cocoa and chocolate industry, it too makes an excellent mulch. The same can be said of chopped, composted straw, composted bark, mushroom compost and loads of muck, all of which are readily available and suitable as soil conditioners.

In Sweden domestic waste is used to fuel power stations, providing energy and subsequently electricity for their national grid, and the ash left behind, which is full of minerals and other nutrients, is utilized on the land. There is talk of doing something similar in this country, and I did hear that it was proposed to build a unit to process chicken or poultry dung to supply the national grid in the eastern counties. Whether or not this ever takes off I suppose we shall find out one day. Of course, one or two pig farmers in this country do actually use the muck from their pigs to provide their homes with electricity, using modern methane digesters, but these are jolly expensive to install and there's not a lot of money in pigs to make this viable. I've always wondered why we couldn't burn all the domestic waste produced in this country instead of using it for landfill. Admittedly, one negative result of this would be the vast amount of carbon dioxide and possibly other gases released which could be harmful to the environment. But then, this stuff is slowly decomposing in huge tips, some of which are on fire anyway, and is giving off carbon dioxide already. Perhaps someone will explain it to me one day.

Liquid manures became very popular in the eighteenth century, particularly on the Continent, and have been so ever since, though until the early 1800s it was not known what magical ingredients caused plants to react to manures and rich dressings. In fact it was only in 1775 that the existence of oxygen was discovered, by an Englishman called Joseph Priestley, and of course this means that photosynthesis was also unknown until then. In the early seventeenth century Francis Bacon decreed that water was the principle source of nourishment for plants and that the earth was only there to support them. He also knew that there were unique substances in the soil that the plant could draw upon, and, although Bacon was unable to identify them, a seventeenth-century Flemish scientist called Jean Baptiste van Helmont supported Bacon's view with practical evidence. He planted a willow tree in an earthenware container, together with 200 pounds (90k.) of soil. The tree weighed 5 pounds (2k.) and was watered accordingly. After five years van Helmont weighed the tree again and found that it had increased in weight to 169 pounds 3 ounces (76.5k.). He could account for all of the 200 pounds (90k.) of soil used except for 2 ounces (48 g.), and as he had only added water he too concluded that this was the sole nutrient of plants. The race was on to find out more, but it wasn't until the discovery of oxygen that everything suddenly fell into perspective, and people realized the importance of carbon, oxygen and hydrogen in plant development.

On the Continent liquid manures were collected from cow stalls and stables, and from privies too. In this country, however, a popular liquid manure was sheep's dung left in water for twelve hours and then passed through a coarse cloth. The liquid was then mixed with a handful of sodium chloride and a couple of pinches of saltpetre. The idea was to put your seeds, ready for sowing, into this mixture and leave them to swell for twenty-four hours, then remove them, allow them to dry and sow them. Unmixed liquid manure was thought to be more effective for the watering of plants. Another unusual fertilizer was based on yeast. It had to be putrid, useless for baker and brewer alike, and was mixed with water and applied as a liquid manure. It was thought to be just right for pineapples, vines and the brassica family, especially cauliflowers, and for potatoes, as a 'pickle' for wheat, and excellent on new-sown turnips. Recently I heard of a firm that was going to use yeast in a similar manner, mixing it with whey and feeding it to pigs. The waste from the pigs was then to be fed to worms to produce compost. It sounds long-winded and complicated and I don't think it has ever taken off. It would also require a huge capital investment at a time of high risk and high interest rates. Today all manner of things are used to make liquid manures – all types of animal dung, old socks and shoes – you name it, someone somewhere has his own distillery at the bottom of the garden.

Saltpetre or potassium nitrate, used mainly for gunpowder, was very popular as a fertilizer from Elizabethan times onwards and it is mentioned in Shakespeare's play *Henry IV*:

> *It was great pity so it was*
> *This villainous saltpetre should be digg'd*
> *Out of the bowels of the harmless earth*

If dissolved in water and used as a liquid manure, it had a marvellous effect on various crops. In the nineteenth century a chap living near a 'petre' house (where saltpetre was refined for use in gunpowder) noticed that all his plants and trees were not only disease-free but also very productive. Today potassium nitrate is expensive and, although it is very high in nitrogen and potash, it is only used on specialized crops, mainly in glasshouse cultivation.

The use of salt on the land goes back to biblical times, but in 1598 Lord Napier took out a patent for improving lands with salt. Francis Bacon recommended it for the garden, and Moses Cook, gardener to the Earl of Essex in 1679, said that salt was like sack (wine) to a young child: 'a little doth a great deal of good'. Used mainly for weed control on gravel paths, it was also employed for the control of slugs and worms, as was salt water which was regarded as a good deterrent for all three. In the eighteenth and nineteenth centuries gardeners started using salt as a stimulant on vegetable crops and found it to be very effective. They even used it on coconut trees in their conservatories, supposing that, as salt would be present in the soil of the coconuts' natural coastal habitat, it would be beneficial. Arguments on the benefits of salt as a manure were aired at horticultural and agricultural societies all over the country. A Mr Bennet of the Bath and West of England Society decreed that salt was not a manure but a stimulant. Mr Collyns of Exeter refuted this statement, saying that salt had had a wondrous effect on the light and sandy arable soils of his region; it restored old pastures and revived the greenswards in gardens, lawns and pleasure grounds. Then why does it kill weeds, asked Mr Bennet. These arguments raged on for over twenty years. I suppose if you spread salt on old pasturelands that had been terribly neglected you would in effect stimulate the soil and the bacteria therein, but it would be a very short-lived benefit. What people didn't realize in those days was that the crops on which they used salt, and which derived direct benefit from it, were mainly brassicas or plants that thrived in coastal areas and utilized the sodium in their growth. Many farmers and gardeners still use salt today for growing brassica crops such as kale, cabbages and Brussels sprouts. Asparagus also thrives on a handful of salt thrown into manure in the autumn.

The gardeners of yesteryear, although doing a great deal of good to the majority of crops through the addition of salt, also lost a lot of land as a result of overdosing the soil, using salt like a manure and putting it on in such vast quantities that it had an adverse effect. One reason that salt might have been preferred to lime as a manure was that huge duties were payable on lime, and only when these were removed in 1827 did lime see a rise in popularity. Other salty materials employed as manure included seaweed, although its use was mainly confined to Cornwall, Devon, parts of Wales and Scotland, where it was considered to enhance the value of the land from ten shillings to twenty shillings an acre. The seaweed was collected from the tidemark and loaded into baskets on donkeys or onto a horse-drawn cart. It was usually allowed to rot for several weeks, and was occasionally mixed with farmyard manure, before being ploughed into the land. On the coast of Normandy, seaweed was collected and charred slightly, rendering it to ashes, before it was sold to farmers on the island of Jersey, where it was known as 'varec'; it proved to be extremely effective in the cultivation of crops there. Seaweed is still used today by crofters in Scotland and Ireland and by farmers in some parts of the West Country, and is also available in a calcified form in which the seaweed is dried, milled and sold in bags. You won't see this material too often in garden centres, but organic farmers tend to use it as it contains a lot of minerals and trace elements and is rich in potash. I wouldn't recommend taking home fresh seaweed in the back of the car, especially if you have a long journey, as it does tend to leave behind a rather powerful odour. However, this didn't deter the Germans from using it for stuffing cushions and mattresses, though this was over a hundred years ago, and our sense of smell has become a little more refined since then. When you handle seaweed on the beach, watch out for tar, which will ruin your clothes. Tar was actually used as a manure by Bishop Berkeley of Cloyne in Ireland in about 1840. A hedge of myrtles was planted by the Bishop who insisted that their root systems be encased in a ball of tar. The hedge, considered to be the finest in all Ireland, was wonderful. Well, with all that carbon round the root systems, I suppose it had a ready supply of food, although I wouldn't recommend this for your plants today. As well as seaweed, coastal farmers considered sea sand to be a very valuable manure, and would go down to the beach at low tide and shovel the wet sand into their carts. It was very beneficial in lightening heavy soils, and of course the salts and minerals it contained offered a good source of nourishment.

Seaweed, or kelp, was also used in the soap-making industry, mainly as fuel for the fires. The ashes were mixed with the refuse from the soap boiler and made a potash-rich manure that was ideal for heavy clays. Soap production seems to have taken place principally in Lancashire, where it was said that farmers commonly applied forty to fifty tons of soaper's waste, as it was known, to the acre. Instead of seaweed, wood was sometimes used as fuel and the ashes treated in a similar way with equal effect.

James Anderson, who farmed at Monks Hill, Aberdeenshire, in 1777, said in his book *Essays Relating to Agriculture and Rural Affairs* that as manure lime 'is of the most universal utility that has yet been discovered'. I am sure that many a gardener and farmer would agree with that statement today. Various forms of lime have been used over the centuries, but it wasn't until the nineteenth century that the benefits of lime were fully understood. One of the commonest forms of it then in use was sulphate of lime, known today as calcium carbonate or carbonate of lime; in the past this material was also referred to as gypsum or plaster of Paris, a name it acquired from the large, naturally occurring deposits of it around Paris. This type of lime, also found in Nottinghamshire, Cheshire and Somerset and in London clay, was burnt down to a white powder and was sold mainly to plasterers. However, it was extensively used in agriculture too, and was found to be especially beneficial to forage crops such as clover and sainfoin. Hydrated lime, or quicklime, which derived from the cement and mortar industry, also became very popular when farmers and gardeners realized its importance in

promoting the fertility of soils. In the past limestone was burnt in a kiln (hence the number of derelict kilns to be seen in limestone areas), and formed a white powder known as calcium oxide. This had to be kept under cover to prevent it absorbing moisture from the air. Today calcium hydroxide, or slaked lime, is used to speed up the composting process. When you mix it with water it gives off heat, which is supposed to spur on the activity of bacteria and encourage decomposition. Sometimes it works, sometimes it doesn't. It does, however, have fast-acting properties and is used mainly in the garden to neutralize the acidity of the soil, though it can be very expensive. In the past farmers often had problems in spreading powdered quicklime on their fields as it caused real dangers to horses if they came into contact with water. If it rained, the horses had to be led off the field very quickly as the lime could burn their fetlocks so severely that animals were sometimes permanently disabled. To counteract the effects of such burning, a bucket of sour milk or whey, in which the horses' feet and legs could be washed to remove all traces of quicklime, was kept close at hand.

Other forms of lime used as manure include crushed or ground lime, which is suitable for all soils and in particular for rich, humus-fed soils. Ground chalk is used on sandy soils and light loams. Ground limestone was first used by a Frenchman called M. du Hamel in the mid 1700s. The marble for a fireplace installed in his house was cut on his lawn, and several months later he noticed that where it had been cut the grass grew far more luxuriantly than on any other part of the lawn. M. du Hamel recorded this observation as a great discovery. He then decided, with good reason, that ground limestone might successfully be employed as a manure. He repeated the experiment several times and found that it never failed to promote fertility on the spot where it had been spread. A cheap manure could be made from ground lime by first raising a platform of earth on the headland or edge of a field. This platform should be about eight feet (2.4m) wide, a foot (30cm) deep and up to forty feet (12m) long. A layer of ground limestone should be placed on this earth and wetted with brine (a salt water solution) and a layer of earth should then be placed on top. This process should be repeated to the height required. After a week the compost should be turned over and mixed. This method was often used in Ireland, where it was reputed to have doubled the potato and cabbage crops and was generally regarded as far superior to horse dung.

Lime water was used in the past to kill worms on lawns and herbaceous borders, and chloride of lime was very effective in destroying pests and insects on trees, and also in preventing pollution arising from the decomposition of vegetable waste. In France chloride of lime was used to preserve the bodies of the poor souls who had committed suicide as it kept them in a fresh state until claimed by their family or friends. It was also employed as a timber preservative.

A once widespread use of calcium carbonate, a crystalline salt found in limestone and chalk, was in the form of marl, which was employed as a fertilizer by farmers in this country before the invasion of the Romans. Marl consisted of a combination of lime and clay and was applied to very sandy soils for the growing of root crops such as mangolds and turnips, which were essential cattle feeds in the eighteenth and nineteenth centuries. In fact it was so vital that farmers used to quote the following verse:

> *He that marls sand*
> *Will soon buy land*
> *But he that marls clay*
> *Throws all away.*

Many acres of barren, sandy heaths in the east of England were reclaimed by using marl. The lime neutralized the acid sand and the clay, with its colloidal properties, combined the fine, sandy particles together. In some places as many as two hundred cart loads of marl were applied per acre. Burnt clay was also used as a manure, and lime kilns were used to carry out this process, which required a great deal of skill and expertise; it was burnt day and night, such was the demand.

Today we use all manner of materials to enrich our soils. Wool waste, known as shoddy, a by-product of the wool industry, has been used over the years, and is sometimes combined today with other waste fabrics such as silk and cotton. Not seen for sale in the garden centres, it is usually sold to those living near the textile factories, and, with a continuing decrease in textile manufacturing in this country, shoddy has seen a dramatic decline over the last twenty-five years. Cotton seed meal was also once used as a manure and now we feed it to our cows, who seem to like it. It's a bit like fluffy, white popcorn and 'pops' when you stand on it. Castor meal, a by-product from the castor oil industry, was also used on the land in the past but isn't seen too often today (although many of you probably remember castor oil and its tumultuous effects very well indeed). Brewers' waste, which consists of spent hops and brewers' grains, has always been popular with gardeners and farmers alike and smells wonderful. Today spent hops are used in compost and as a manure on the land while brewers' grains are fed to cattle. We have even fed them to our cows, so whoever said that cows eat only grass can think again; our cows certainly have a wide variety of vegetarian foods, in fact more than some restaurant menus offer.

So many waste products abound in our country today and yet there is almost always a use for them somewhere. I hope you have enjoyed this penultimate chapter, and that it has perhaps brought back some childhood memories or induced ideas for the future.

CHAPTER SIX

IN THE END . . .

Money is like muck, not good except it be spread!
FRANCIS BACON (1561–1626)

*H*ow true the above saying is. And over four hundred years later we are taking Francis Bacon's words more literally than he ever intended them. Instead of burning old and tatty banknotes, the Bank of England has decided to compost them, so to coin another phrase, where there's muck there's brass. I did enquire as to how one obtained this marvellous waste material as I was extremely interested in using it on the farm. Oh well, money isn't everything.

In this final chapter on muck, weird and wonderful alternative uses are given for those of you fortunate enough to have a compost heap at the bottom of the garden, and even for those of you who don't have a garden at all. You just wouldn't believe the uses to which muck and worms can be put. But then, having read this book, you just might. Did you know for instance, that dried sewage sludge attires the rich and famous in the guise of jewellery? Once it is mixed with water it can be moulded to any shape, painted a multitude of colours and then fired, just as you would make a piece of pottery. Through the ages, of course, many a cottage wall has been built of muck, providing insulation and warmth, and buffalo dung (or chips as the American Indians call them) and dried cow pats have been used as a fuel for fires. The heat of dung in the process of decomposition has been utilized by gardeners for centuries in hotbeds, enabling them to grow not only tropical plants but also mushrooms all the year round. The methane gas given off from muck can be used in methane digesters to provide electricity. Rabbit dung; duck muck; cricket droppings; lion muck (which is very efficient at deterring deer in your garden and a darn sight cheaper than keeping your own pride of lions); other animal dung from the zoo, known as zoo do: you name it and someone is making a compost out of it somewhere.

But what would happen if there wasn't any muck? Well, that problem was solved by a friend of mine. Although she had plenty of the stuff lying around, she decided to use her beloved, recently deceased cat as garden compost. Wanting to commemorate this treasured cat, and at the same time to make the best possible use of its remains, my friend decided to bury it in the garden and plant a tree on top. Unfortunately, this cat decided to pass away in the summer and summer is not a good time to plant trees. Reluctant to be defeated, however, she put her dead cat in the freezer – not in a bag or a box or in tinfoil – she just plonked it on top of everything else and waited for the autumn when she could plant her commemorative tree. Well, as you can imagine, when someone was sent out unwittingly to fetch ice cream they were surprised and horrified to find this beloved cat frozen to death in the freezer. How does one break the news to its owner? Anyway, autumn arrived, a spot was chosen in the garden, the cat was thawed out and duly placed in the bottom of the hole and a lilac tree was planted on top. What a wonderful way to remember your cat. Just think of all that goodness giving life to something else, even after death. Though it does make you wonder what you'll find in your friends' freezers if something dies at the wrong time of year.

As children we had numerous pets, most of which seemed to come to a sticky end, but at least some of them finished up fertilizing the vegetable garden. Goldie the goldfish was sucked up in the hoover by my young brother; Tommy the budgerigar suffered a heart attack after my mother decided to hoover out his

cage instead of just removing the sandpaper in the bottom; Percy the pigeon came to a mysterious end (and I think he was cremated) after he pooped over everything in the airing cupboard. The friend with the dead cat also lost her beloved hunter, and when he was sent off (we don't mention where) she asked if she could have one of his legs to remember him by. This leg was not put in the freezer, I might add, but was placed in another hole in the garden with a tree on top. Unfortunately, this tree hasn't done too well, but then, if the leg was put in whole, it would be a very long time before the goodness from the bones seeped into the soil. It should really have been chopped up into little pieces for immediate effect. I just wonder what else she's got buried in the garden. There was a lovely story I heard recently about two elderly sisters who lived together; one of them died and the other sister put her body on the compost heap, saying that that was what she wanted and it was where she deserved to go anyway. I can see where I'm going to end up.

If you have read Chapter Four about worms, then you will realize how important they are for the soil, but I wonder if you know of their other uses. When worm farming was introduced on a commercial basis in this country in the 1980s, worms were bred on an experimental farm to see which species produced the most protein and how viable this enterprise might be. Researchers there were looking for a high protein product to replace all the soya and corn that was fed to animals and, since worms provide on average seventy per cent of their dried body weight in protein, they seemed to be the ideal choice. The idea was to breed millions of these worms, separate them from their bedding, dry them, pulverize them into powder and use this in animal feed. However, a dried worm doesn't add up to much and I calculated that you would have to cover an area the size of Wales with worms in order to feed the animals in this country just for a month. And I don't think the Welsh would be too happy about that. The scientists on this experimental farm eventually rejected the enterprise as unviable and switched their attention to the casts that these worms produced, convinced that they were on to something. Worm compost was to be the way forward. And we all know what happened to that.

However, the outcome of all this is that a scheme is under consideration in some Third World countries to breed certain large varieties of worm and use them as a high protein source in biscuits to be fed to refugees. In Japan there is a festival in the autumn, or

so I have been told, at which a delicacy called Japanese worm pie is served; one has to remember that worms in Japan can be twice the size of worms in England and full of protein, so you have really got something to get your teeth into. In the Philippines poverty is so extreme that children are sent out onto the huge municipal rubbish dumps to forage for worms, which are then taken home and made into soups and stews. In New Zealand worms are considered by the Maoris to be quite a delicacy and are eaten in their raw state, along with other creepy crawlies. In South Africa a favourite is fried worms, and in Britain a speciality with the marines is worm omelette. Now I have never eaten worm omelette, but I have it on first-hand authority that, before these rough tough fellows are sent out into the big unknown and have to survive on next to nothing, they are given the low-down on what they should eat in the natural environment in order to survive. And worms, because they are so plentiful, come top of the list. But to introduce them to these chaps, they first make an omelette, with lots and lots of salt and pepper, then get hold of Dirty Harry, chop him into little bits, throw him in, et voila! Now, should you get stuck on the Brecon Beacons, with no chance of help for twenty-four hours and not a morsel in your glovebox, do not despair. Just think of all that food around you. All you have to do is catch it. (A TV programme on worm charming is now a necessity.) Once you have caught your worms, the larger the better, I suggest that you soak them in a puddle of water. Do NOT soak them in the car radiator as the antifreeze will kill you before it kills the worm. Remember, Dirty Harry has been ingesting a lot of dirt, and soaking him in water washes this out. There's nothing worse than having sand in your food. Ughh! It's like seaside holidays all over again.

Other uses of worms for the less desperate once included poultices for both human and animal complaints such as gall stones, piles, fevers, jaundice and smallpox. Worms were eaten to cure impotence, to induce milk and enable mothers to breast-feed their children and as a means of pregnancy testing. This was carried out by injecting urine into the worm; smears taken from the worm's seminal vesicles – part of its sexual organs – before and after injection revealed spermatogenesis or the production of mature male cells. This test was found to be ninety per cent accurate but no, I definitely wouldn't recommend it. Scientists consider that worms might contain vital substances to help relieve rheumatism and bronchial troubles, and have also used them to test for carcinogenic properties. Poor old Dirty Harry: he has even been ground up for toothpaste, applied as hair restorer and cooked in a sealed jam jar in the centre of a dung heap to produce worm oil, which was apparently applied to the joints to alleviate pain, a link perhaps with his recent connection with rheumatism.

Well I think that just about covers it: everything you wanted to know about muck and probably more. *Magic Muck* has certainly been great fun to write and brought a lot of memories flooding back. I only hope you have had as much fun reading it, and perhaps trying out my composting methods and recipes, and that you are now on the way to becoming a Lady (or Lord) Muck of the future.

CHARLIE WORM

I had a little invertebrate friend, his name was Charlie Worm,
I took him everywhere, I did, but he didn't half make people
    squirm;
They thought he was wet and cold, you see,
They just didn't understand,
But Charlie Worm was a hero to me,
The greatest chap in the land.

I fed him dainty morsels and cow pats nice and dry,
Steaming manure on a frosty morning from dung heaps up to the
    sky,
He devoured the cow pats by the hour,
The dung heaps by the day,
But the biggest allure was the steaming manure
And from that I couldn't keep him away.

He grew and grew did Charlie until he could grow no more,
And then one morning I found his tail lying cold on the concrete
    floor,
For that nasty creature, Villainous Fred,
A rival company mole,
Had cut him in two and left him for dead
Before dragging his head down his hole.

I buried the corpse of poor Charlie Worm, shrivelled and far from
    whole,
(The head is the end that makes him squirm and the tastiest part
    for a mole),
Now, many months on, I often think of my friend
In the compost he helped me to sell,
And would like him to know that, sad though his end,
His offspring are doing rather well.

INDEX

MEDICAL™

Large Print

Titles for the next six months…

January

SINGLE DAD, OUTBACK WIFE	Amy Andrews
A WEDDING IN THE VILLAGE	Abigail Gordon
IN HIS ANGEL'S ARMS	Lynne Marshall
THE FRENCH DOCTOR'S MIDWIFE BRIDE	Fiona Lowe
A FATHER FOR HER SON	Rebecca Lang
THE SURGEON'S MARRIAGE PROPOSAL	Molly Evans

February

THE ITALIAN GP'S BRIDE	Kate Hardy
THE CONSULTANT'S ITALIAN KNIGHT	Maggie Kingsley
HER MAN OF HONOUR	Melanie Milburne
ONE SPECIAL NIGHT…	Margaret McDonagh
THE DOCTOR'S PREGNANCY SECRET	Leah Martyn
BRIDE FOR A SINGLE DAD	Laura Iding

March

THE SINGLE DAD'S MARRIAGE WISH	Carol Marinelli
THE PLAYBOY DOCTOR'S PROPOSAL	Alison Roberts
THE CONSULTANT'S SURPRISE CHILD	Joanna Neil
DR FERRERO'S BABY SECRET	Jennifer Taylor
THEIR VERY SPECIAL CHILD	Dianne Drake
THE SURGEON'S RUNAWAY BRIDE	Olivia Gates

MILLS & BOON®
Pure reading pleasure

1207 LP 2P P1 Medical

MEDICAL™

 *Large Print* —

April

THE ITALIAN COUNT'S BABY	Amy Andrews
THE NURSE HE'S BEEN WAITING FOR	Meredith Webber
HIS LONG-AWAITED BRIDE	Jessica Matthews
A WOMAN TO BELONG TO	Fiona Lowe
WEDDING AT PELICAN BEACH	Emily Forbes
DR CAMPBELL'S SECRET SON	Anne Fraser

May

THE MAGIC OF CHRISTMAS	Sarah Morgan
THEIR LOST-AND-FOUND FAMILY	Marion Lennox
CHRISTMAS BRIDE-TO-BE	Alison Roberts
HIS CHRISTMAS PROPOSAL	Lucy Clark
BABY: FOUND AT CHRISTMAS	Laura Iding
THE DOCTOR'S PREGNANCY BOMBSHELL	Janice Lynn

June

CHRISTMAS EVE BABY	Caroline Anderson
LONG-LOST SON: BRAND-NEW FAMILY	Lilian Darcy
THEIR LITTLE CHRISTMAS MIRACLE	Jennifer Taylor
TWINS FOR A CHRISTMAS BRIDE	Josie Metcalfe
THE DOCTOR'S VERY SPECIAL CHRISTMAS	Kate Hardy
A PREGNANT NURSE'S CHRISTMAS WISH	Meredith Webber

MILLS & BOON®
Pure reading pleasure

1207 LP 2P P2 Medical